Galleries of Garden Plants

THE BEST OF
FINE GARDENING

Galleries of Garden Plants

The Taunton Press

Cover photos: top left, top right and bottom left,
Chris Curless; top center and bottom center, Mark Kane;
bottom right, Susan Kahn

Back-cover photos: left and right, Chris Curless; top center,
Mark Kane; bottom center, Renée Beaulieu

Taunton
BOOKS & VIDEOS
for fellow enthusiasts

First printing: 1996
Printed in the United States of America

A Fine Gardening Book

Fine Gardening® is a trademark of The Taunton Press, Inc.,
registered in the U.S. Patent and Trademark Office.

The Taunton Press
63 South Main Street
Box 5506
Newtown, CT 06470-5506

Library of Congress Cataloging-in-Publication Data

Galleries of garden plants.
        p.   cm. — (The Best of Fine gardening)
      "A Fine gardening book" — T.p. verso.
      Includes index.
      ISBN 1-56158-139-9
      1. Plants, Ornamental. 2. Landscape gardening. I. Fine
gardening. II. Series.
SB407.G3235   1996   95-45510
    635.9 — dc20   CIP

Contents

Introduction

The last time you had some open space in your garden and were thinking of how to fill it, how did you choose your plants? Did you have an idea of the *kind* of plant you were looking for but didn't know enough to call it by name? Were you looking for something with golden leaves, or a fast-growing vine, but didn't know where to start? If you're not a walking plant encyclopedia, you might wonder where to turn. And that's the reasoning behind this latest collection from *Fine Gardening* magazine.

In this beautifully photographed volume, expert home gardeners and horticulturists look at plant selection from the point of view of classes of plants that fill a certain role or perform a specific function within the context of the planting site. We've grouped plants by color, season of bloom, length of bloom and several other characteristics. The emphasis here is on giving you the right information and perspective to be able to select plants that fit your own garden.

The articles in this collection are especially helpful and inspiring because they are the work of enthusiasts who actually grow these plants themselves. Sharing their hard-won experience, the authors tell you how to succeed with each variety.

The editors of *Fine Gardening* hope you'll find this book useful when it comes time to select plants, and all you know is that you'd like something that blooms in the fall, for at least six weeks....

"The Best of *Fine Gardening*" series collects articles from back issues of *Fine Gardening* magazine. A note on p. 96 gives the date of first publication for each article; product availability, suppliers' addresses and prices may have changed since then. This book is the tenth in the series.

(Left) In bright contrast to surrounding green foliage, the silver leaves of two dusty miller cultivars light up a border in late spring. A close look at a dusty miller leaf (above) reveals that its silver color comes from a dense webbing of tiny white hairs that almost obscure the green surface. Gray and silver leaves bring unity, drama and variety to a garden all season long.

A Celebration of Silver Leaves

Plants with bright foliage enliven green gardens

by Panayoti Kelaidis

A real Garden of Eden lingers in the memory of most gardeners—whether it's a courtyard we glimpsed through the chink of a wall as a child or a dazzling public garden visited in middle age. My look at Eden came ten years ago on a visit to a garden organized not just for a few weeks or months of color, but for beauty all year round. On that late winter day, a symphony of foliage engaged my eyes more colorfully and vibrantly than any arrangement of flowers I had ever seen. The most prominent and instructive feature of the garden was light-colored foliage—gray and silver leaves—which wove through the shades of green, making the garden glow even under overcast skies.

Designing with silver and gray

Since that visit, I have become convinced that foliage is the foundation of a good garden, and that no garden is complete without at least a splash of gray or silver to extend its range of colors. Because gray and silver contrast with surrounding leaves and flowers, they create dramatic accents in a garden. Their strongly reflective quality makes them look as if they are caught in a shaft of sunlight, an effect you can harness to direct the eyes of your visitors.

Gray- and silver-leaved plants play a variety of roles in garden design. They act as a foil for the plants you put next to them. Most colors, from bright to muted, show off more effectively against a clean silver background than they do against green. The flashing scarlet of an annual verbena, for example, appears even brighter against the fleecy white leaves of an artemisia.

Silver and gray foliage also serves as a harmonizer in the garden. Strident colors, such as hot pink or bright yellow, can appear discordant right next to one another. But they combine so well with silver and gray that silver and gray become effective buffers, preventing jarring combinations.

There are as many shades of silver and gray foliage as there are of green. The range goes from almost white through gray to blue-gray, allowing you to command attention or create subtle highlights. Bright white or satiny silver foliage tends to stand out in a garden, while darker gray or blue-gray tones retreat from the eyes.

It is hard to go too far wrong in placing silver and gray plants in the garden, but I believe they are best used sparingly to achieve specific effects. In the Rock Alpine Garden at the Denver Botanic Gardens, where I am curator, we use light-colored-foliage plants in groups to act as sentinels or focal points. You can also try them in the forefront of plantings to delineate the garden from its surroundings. Or use gray and silver to reinforce the lines of a wall or a walk, repeating architectural rhythms.

Not just for dry spots

What makes leaves silver or gray? Most gray or silver plants get their coloring from countless tiny hairs that cover the leaves; under the hairs, the leaves are quite green. Botanists believe that for many gray- and silver-leaved plants, the hairs are an adaptation to dry conditions. The hairs protect the leaves by diffusing and reflecting sunlight, reducing water-loss by acting like miniature white umbrellas. But not all gray- or silver-leaved plants prefer drought. Many are alpines, native to mountain slopes where their roots are often drenched in moisture. Gray is also common in plants that grow on moist mountain-sides in New Zealand, South Africa and South America. Even among natives of the Mediterranean, where summers are dry, there are gray-leaved plants, such as lamb's-ears, that grow well in the relatively wet Northeast.

While gray- and silver-leaved plants can be surprisingly adaptable, they do have their limits. You can guess that a furry plant will grow well in a sunny spot where drainage is good. It may also tolerate or even prefer light shade, provided it gets half a day's sunshine. But few gray- or silver-leaved plants prosper in the deadly combination of heat, humidity and poor drainage common in the Southeast. There are exceptions, though, and I'll tell you about them.

A gallery of silver-leaved plants

In catalogs and garden centers, you will encounter a good number of plants with silver or gray leaves. Here and in the next article ("More Garden Silver," pp. 12-15), I'll tell you about some of the light-colored foliage plants—both tried-and-true and up-and-coming—that I have enjoyed growing in my garden. (See Sources on p. 10.)

Dusty miller—One winter day I noticed in a neighbor's garden a shrubby, silver-leaved plant that I couldn't place. The cut-edged leaves grew in whorls around stout stems, and the plant formed a robust mound that glowed all winter. I grew more and more puzzled each time I drove by, curious to know what wedding cake of a perennial this marvelous thing

A winding collar of gleaming lamb's-ears wraps the edge of a perennial border.

not flower. The second year, and every year thereafter, it forms a mound 2 ft. tall and about as wide (like the plant I couldn't identify) and bears small yellow flowers off and on all summer. Though attractive, the flowers play second fiddle to the foliage.

Lamb's-ears—Lamb's-ears (*Stachys byzantina, S. lanata*) occupies a special place in many of our memories. Like shooting stars, lilies-of-the-valley and snapdragons, it captures the imagination of children. I will never forget my disappointment when I stroked the ears of my first real lamb: the animal was irresistible, but its fur felt like steel wool compared to the heavenly softness of vegetable lamb's-ears.

The leaves of lamb's-ears form a repeatedly branching mat that can be divided endlessly. In June, 2-ft. tall flower stems rise over the leaves like stout pokers. They are covered with gray hairs and capped with small, pink flowers that barely extrude from the fur. Many gardeners feel that the flower stalks make the plants look as if they need a haircut. For them there is 'Silver Carpet', a cultivar that never blooms. It is as close to plush carpeting as you can expect in a garden.

Lamb's-ears may be the most versatile of silver edging plants. Many gardeners use it as a cool splash of color in the front of a border, but it also makes an effective edging between perennials and lawn (see photo at left) or a silver collar along paths.

Lamb's-ears is hardy to Zone 4 (-30°F). In warmer climes, its woolly leaves may continue to brighten the garden through much of winter.

Licorice plant—For many gardeners, helichrysums are strawflowers grown in the cutting garden, but there are also helichrysums grown for their lustrous silver or gray foliage. Among the plants available in the nursery trade, the licorice plant (*Helichrysum petiolatum*) is the most striking (see photo on facing page). It bears fragrant, furry leaves the size of postage stamps on long, sprawling stems. (The leaves are not the source of licorice flavoring.) The leaves are silvery on one side and grayer on the other, a two-tone effect that adds much to the plant's allure and persists when stems are harvested and dried for flower arrangements.

In the garden, the licorice plant is an ideal filler—it spreads nicely to occupy empty spaces left by ephemerals such as spring bulbs or to give

was. I finally dragged a friend over to share my discovery. To my chagrin he said we were looking at dusty miller, a common plant that I should have recognized. He still smirks whenever he says "dusty miller" in my presence.

I had always thought of dusty miller (*Senecio cineraria*) as a straggly annual, usually planted to mediate the struggle between screaming orange marigolds and purple-red petunias. Although it plays this role well, it also deserves a place as a highlight in perennial and shrub borders (see photo on p. 8). It is reliably perennial where drainage is good and winter temperatures don't drop much below -10°F (USDA Hardiness Zone 6). And because its silver finery stands up well in the face of chilly temperatures, dusty miller makes a good companion for evergreen shrubs and ground covers.

Dusty miller is an example of a silver-leaved plant that grows well in almost every part of North America. It thrives in the steamy South and shines through cool Northern summers. The first year from seeds, dusty miller grows only about 1 ft. tall and does

SOURCES

The numbers after each plant refer to the mail-order sources that carry it.

Dusty miller (*Senecio cineraria*) 2

Lamb's-ears (*Stachys byzantina*) 1,2,3,4
Non-flowering lamb's-ears
(*S. byzantina* 'Silver Carpet') 1

Licorice plant
(*Helichrysum petiolatum*) 3

Silver sage (*Salvia argentea*) 2,4

Snow-in-summer
(*Cerastium tomentosum*) 1,2,4

1. **Carroll Gardens,** 444 East Main Street, P.O. Box 310, Westminster, MD 21158, 410-848-5422. Catalog $2, deductible from first order. Plants.

2. **The Flowery Branch,** P.O. Box 1330, Flowery Branch, GA 30542, 706-536-8380. Catalog $2 for a 2-year subscription. Seeds.

3. **Richters,** 357 Hwy. 47, Goodwood, Ontario, Canada L0C 1A0, 416-640-6677. Catalog $2 (U.S. funds). Plants.

4. **White Flower Farm,** Rte. 63, Litchfield, CT 06759-0050, 203-496-9600. Catalog free. Plants.

The woolly gray leaves and furry stems of the licorice plant weave through an orange-flowered *Zinnia angustifolia*. Gray- and silver-leaved plants can intensify other colors.

Reference books insist that silver sage lives only two years, but I know a specimen in Colorado that has persisted for 20 years—surely the record for the longest-lived biennial. You can encourage plants to carry on by removing the wiry, yard-long bloom stalks that appear in mid-spring after the helmet-shaped, white flowers fade. As insurance, leave one stalk to set seeds. Silver sage is easy to raise from seeds sown indoors well before the last frost. It's hardy to Zone 5 (-20°F).

Snow-in-summer—If you have a sunny space and want to fill it with the whitest of foliage, plant snow-in-summer (*Cerastium tomentosum*). Its narrow, 1-in. long leaves on prostrate stems form a tight, fine-textured mat. Only when the starry white flowers open in May and June do you see that the leaves are not quite white but creamy.

Snow-in-summer needs room to perform. A single plant can spread to become a carpet a yard or more across on any soil softer than concrete. I like it in bold drifts at the front of sunny borders or as a sinuous edging to a bed, where its white foliage can provide a foil for magenta, blue or scarlet flowers. Snow-in-summer is cold-hardy to Zone 3 (-40°F).

Try painting your borders with silver and gray to enrich the infinite, subtle shades of green. You will be well on the way to recreating Eden. □

Panayoti Kelaidis gardens in Denver, Colorado, and is the curator of the Rock Alpine Garden at Denver Botanic Gardens.

substance to a corner of early-flowering lilies after they bloom. It also makes a wonderful container plant.

The licorice plant is a tender shrub. In mild-winter climates (Zone 8 or warmer), it can grow 4 ft. tall and equally wide, bearing button-like, papery white flowers in early summer. Gardeners in temperate climates can grow the licorice plant as an annual. In a single season, its ground-hugging stems grow about 3 ft. long. At the approach of cool weather, you can root tip cuttings indoors in a light soil mix or dig up a plant and overwinter it on a sunny windowsill. It also numbers among the few gray- and silver-leaved plants that thrive in the South.

Silver sage—Silver sage (*Salvia argentea*) represents the ultimate in foliage extravagance. It looks like a small zucchini plant dressed in an ermine coat. The neatly combed swirls of fur on the 1-ft. long, triangular leaves are irresistible—you *have* to stroke them.

Any plant with such large and sensuous white foliage needs to be placed with a little care. Silver sage has a presence in the garden similar to that of sculpture. It looks best abutting a path, where its bold, low-growing leaves can be admired conveniently and where it isn't apt to upstage its neighbors. No matter where you put it, expect children and hedonists to make a bee-line for it and quietly stroke its giant, shaggy-dog leaves.

The white hairs flowing over the leaves of a silver sage make the plant appear to glow.

A carpet of snow-in-summer in bloom cascades over a stone wall. After the flowers fade, the foliage shines on in contrast to more predictable shades of green.

A bright mass of *Artemisia ludoviciana* tumbles over a planting of pink alliums like a frothy, silver wave. Gray- and silver-leaved plants can add striking highlights to green gardens.

More Garden Silver

Gray-leaved plants add light and warmth to the garden

by Panayoti Kelaidis

Ornamental gardening in America is very much a stepchild of the gardening that's been going on for centuries in the wet, green lands of Western Europe, particularly the British Isles. So for many people, gardening means expanses of green lawn, lushness and the misty green backdrop of a maritime climate. But visit England today, and you'll be struck by the rich symphony of foliage colors—especially gray and silver—that brighten England's best gardens. It's as if English gardeners wish to capture some of the sun and warmth of the Mediterranean coast, where gray and silver dominate the landscape. We North American gardeners need to take yet another lesson from our horticultural homeland. Green is well and good, but it's even better when spiced with the exotic sheen of silver-leaved plants.

Gray and silver leaves are an adaptation to heat and drought. Plants that thrive in the shade and in cloudy regions spread their chlorophyll out widely to catch as much sunlight as they can—hence the broad leaves of hostas and rhubarbs. But plants from the Mediterranean, the dry plains of Asia or the western United States—places where the sun burns incessantly for weeks on end—often have small leaves protected by thick coverings of wax or dense coats of white hairs, which give them a gray or silver cast.

Since most gray- and silver-leaved plants come from warm regions and

The scalloped, gray-felt leaves of *Marrubium incanum*, an ornamental relative of common horehound, rise past a branch of the old rose 'Violacée'.

have a fine texture, you must place them with care. Apply them in your garden as an artist uses highlights in a painting—in the foreground, on the edges and on reflective surfaces. Use gray- and silver-leaved plants wherever it is hot in your garden or where you would like the effect of warmth—near patios, against foundations or in sunny nooks. The brighter and sunnier the picture you wish to paint, the more appropriate silver foliage will be.

In the previous article ("A Celebration of Silver Leaves," pp. 8-11), I

described a number of gray- and silver-leaved plants and how to use them in the garden. Here I'll tell you about several more— all of them perennials that I grow in the Rock Alpine Garden at the Denver Botanic Garden, where I am curator. You may find many of these plants at local garden centers. Others you may have to order by mail (see Sources on p. 15).

Frosted yarrows

For most gardeners, yarrow means *Achillea millefolium*, one of the most widespread of all wildflowers. The common yarrow is so vigorous—and so green—that many gardeners don't realize that there are yarrows with silver leaves. These yarrows are much more mild-mannered, and they keep their foliage fresh all year long.

One of my favorite silver-leaved yarrows is *A. ageratifolia*, a dwarf ground cover that forms tight mats an inch or so tall. The foliage looks like narrow fern fronds dipped in white frosting. The flowers, tiny white daisies on stems 4 in. to 6 in. tall, come in May and June, completely obscuring the foliage for several weeks. Each flower stem looks like a perfect boutonniere of marguerite daisies.

This Greek or Serbian yarrow is hardy to USDA Hardiness Zone 4 (-30°F) and grows either in full sun or part shade, as long as the soil is well drained. It fares well, once established, with very little rainfall, and like other silverlings, seems longer lived if fertilized with a light hand.

For a gray-leaved yarrow with enough presence to occupy the second rank in a perennial border, consider *A.* 'Moonshine'. This popular hybrid

The yellow flower heads of the hybrid yarrow 'Moonshine' rise over its fern-like gray leaves along the edge of a rock outcropping in late spring. When the long-lasting flowers finally fade, the foliage adds welcome contrast to the standard garden greens for the rest of the year.

forms a tufted mound of feathery gray foliage. In late spring, the mound sends up 12-in. to 18-in. tall stems bearing flat-topped clusters of flowers. The flowers are a soft moonlight yellow that blends easily with practically any other hue. The flowers last for many weeks—from late May into July—then yield the stage to the gray leaves, which last well into winter.

'Moonshine' will glow in a warm, sunny spot throughout much of North America. It tolerates winter cold into Zone 3 (-40°F) and endures a fair measure of heat and humidity, although, like most gray-leaved plants, it soon rots in the Deep South.

Powdery pussy-toes
Gardeners can become so obsessed with the rare and the exquisite that they take for granted everyday plants that contribute to the garden in simpler ways. Pussy-toes (Antennaria spp.) grows over much of the northern hemisphere, and abundantly here in the Rockies. The plant is utter simplicity—

The dusty rosettes of pussy-toes, a diminutive native ground cover, are dwarfed by a thumb and forefinger.

a collection of lax rosettes, each consisting of three or four 1-in. long gray leaves clothed in fine, gray hairs. The rosettes spread to form a mat of lovely symmetry year round. In spring, they produce clusters of flowers, which really do resemble the pads of a cat's paw, on stalks rising 3 in. to 8 in. in height. The flower color varies from gray to nearly white, but a few selections are rosy pink or dark crimson.

The dusty foliage of pussy-toes looks lovely spreading in the cracks between stepping stones. It drapes dramatically when planted on rock walls, and also looks delightful as an edging in the drier parts of the garden.

Pussy-toes lives longest in full sun on dry, gravelly soils (it falters in wet, cool conditions). Plants are hardy to Zone 3, and benefit from being divided and moved from time to time.

Gray and silver lace
When a gardener reaches the artemisia stage of gardening, you know you have a hard-bitten case. Even

hostas have blossoms that are fetching in certain lights, but members of the sagebrush and wormwood genus (Artemisia spp.) are usually more attractive out of bloom than in flower. Artemisias are the garden equivalent of lace, where foliage is reduced to the finest filigree and glows white in bright day or evening light.

There are artemisias to fit any garden—tall ones, prostrate ground covers, mound-formers and shrubs. For many years now, A. schmidtiana 'Silver Mound' has been one of the best selling perennials. It makes a silvery white, symmetrical mound 10 in. to 12 in. tall and 18 in. across. It grows in a wide variety of sites and soils, and can be used much as dusty miller is used—to edge a border or provide a foil for bright colors. It is hardy to Zone 4.

The best known of the larger wormwoods is A. ludoviciana (see photo on p. 12), named for Louisiana in its very widest Louisiana-Purchase sense. King Louis XIV himself never shone more brilliantly than this glistening artemisia in its various royal manifestations. ('Silver King' and 'Silver Queen' are the most common cultivars.) It forms a lax, shrubby mound of powdery white leaves, reaching up to 4 ft. tall. Few plants create such drama in a border as this native.

Unfortunately, 'Silver King' and 'Silver Queen' have a thoroughly plebeian tendency to spread from the roots, especially in rich soil. Slow them down by planting them in the hottest, driest corner of the garden and forcing them to tough it out with such fellow thugs as gooseneck loosestrife (Lysimachia clethroides). Both cultivars are hardy to Zone 4.

If you'd prefer to brighten your garden with a large artemisia you won't have to chase, look to 'Powis Castle'. 'Powis Castle' is a shrubby hybrid that appeared spontaneously at the great English garden for which it is named. The white filigree mass of foliage, 18 in. tall, provides the perfect foil for any bright flower. The royal blue-purple of Salvia × superba, the scarlet of a dahlia, the orange of a California poppy never look half as vibrant as they do juxtaposed against the furious silver-white of 'Powis Castle'.

'Powis Castle' is more tender than the stalwart artemisias I've described, perhaps reaching its cold limit in

The silver filigree of *Artemisia* 'Powis Castle' foliage washes into the scarlet blades of Japanese blood grass (*Imperata cylindrica* 'Red Baron'), creating a dramatic combination.

SOURCES

The plants described in this article are available from several mail-order nurseries. The following is a selection of sources which carry, among them, all of the plants. The numbers after each plant refer to the sources that carry it.

Achillea ageratifolia **4**

A. x 'Moonshine' **1,2,3**

Antennaria dioica **1,2,3,4**

Artemisia 'Powis Castle' **1,2,3,**

A. 'Silver King' and 'Silver Queen' **1,2,3**

A. 'Silver Mound' **1,2,3**

Marrubium incanum **2**

---

1. Carroll Gardens, 444 East Main Street, P.O. Box 310, Westminster, MD 21158, 410-848-5422. Catalog $2, deductible from first order.

2. Dabney Herbs, P.O. Box 22061, Louisville, KY 40252, 502-893-5198. Catalog $2.

3. Forestfarm, 990 Tetherow Road, Williams, OR 97544-9599, 503-846-7269. Catalog $3.

4. Siskiyou Rare Plant Nursery, 2825 Cummings Road, Medford, OR 97501, 503-772-6846. Catalog $2, deductible from first order.

Zone 6 (-10°F). But it roots easily from late-season cuttings, so you need never be without it if you have a cool, sunny windowsill. 'Powis Castle' makes up for its relative tenderness by faring much better in the hot and humid South than do most other silver-leaved plants. It thrives in full sun and well-drained soil and benefits from irrigation in long dry spells.

A bright and shining herb

Today herbs such as lavender and chives are as likely to be found in a flower border as in an herb garden. The common horehound (Marrubium vulgare) is just a bit too rangy to justify a spot in most people's borders, but it has highly ornamental relatives. M. incanum is among the most silvery (see photo on p. 13). It has the rounded, scalloped leaves characteristic of the genus, but they are thicker and more deeply felted with gray hairs.

M. incanum produces a 1-ft. tall mound of gray leaves. It never overwhelms its neighbors, and it looks good in my garden most of the calendar year. I like it on a wall or between rocks in the rock garden. It also can be used to edge a perennial border much the way lamb's-ears can. Because M. incanum tolerates more shade than most gray-leaved plants do, try it, too, as an underplanting for shrubs and roses.

Alas, the small, tubular flowers of M. incanum aren't nearly as attractive as the foliage. Opening in whorls in late spring, they vary from tepid gray to greenish white. Once my horehounds come into full bloom, I usually take the shears to them, for they are primarily foliage plants and utterly worth growing for the leaves alone.

M. incanum is of the easiest culture in the garden. It tolerates heat and drought, but it does best in a rich soil where it receives occasional watering in drier summers. M. incanum is hardy to Zone 5 (-20°F).

Gray- and silver-leaved plants are the highlights of the garden. Spread them through borders and along paths as you would arrange moonbeams on a moonlit night to glow at your feet and warm the scene even when the sun is dark and nearly forgotten. ∎

Panayoti Kelaidis is the curator of the Rock Alpine Garden at Denver Botanic Gardens, Denver, Colorado.

Gold-Leaved Plants Keep the Hues of Spring

Careful plant selection and siting gild a garden

Enduring gold: Yellow hues of spring foliage can last all summer when you grow gold-leaved plants. Here, Gold stripe bamboo shades a bench and pots of *Chrysanthemum parthenium* 'Aureum' in a garden designed by the author. Yellow-flowered *Inula ensifolia* accents the yellow-green foliage of 'Gold Mound' spiraea and 'Gold Leaf' forsythia behind it. 'Aurea' moneywort gilds the brickwork.

Photo: Gary Mottau

by Gary Koller

In spring, the unfurling leaves of many plants display a rich palette. Their exuberant and translucent tints of yellow, gold, pink, red, burgundy and bronze are rich hues that change quickly, however. In a matter of weeks, their color often matures to a monotonous shade of green.

As a gardener, a garden designer and teacher of a course called "Plants in Design" at Harvard University's Graduate School of Design, I have trained my eyes to notice and enjoy the delicate colors of spring foliage. The colors that most captivate me are lime-, yellow- and gold-greens, which are most effective at providing relief from the darker greens.

To capture and hold these shades of spring in my own garden, I've discovered an array of plants that keep their golden hues into summer (see photo on p. 18). (For a selection of plants, see "Hardy gold-leaved plants for the garden" on p. 19.) I will explain how to use these gold-leaved plants to light up a landscape.

Brighten dark areas

Extend the day—My enchantment with these plants arises largely from the fact that they are especially effective at dusk. Their golden leaves catch the failing light of day, causing the plants to glow as if they were the ghosts of twilight (see photo at right). By incorporating gold-leaved plants into a garden, I can extend its potential for enjoyment into the evening.

Sunshine on a cloudy day—The golden glow of a scattering of these plants throughout a garden relieves the gloom of cloudy and overcast days by providing an illusion of dappled sunlight. This principle is useful in climates where the days are often overcast, areas such as the Pacific Northwest.

Coloring shade gardens—In shaded sites, there often is not enough sun for plants to achieve flowering. But many gold-leaved plants, which thrive

Extend the day: A golden-leaved grass, *(Hakonechloa macra* 'Aureola') reflects the warm light of sundown.

in shade, make good substitutes. The hue of their foliage brightens dark garden corners and adds color to them.

Painting a garden in gold

Gold-leaved plants look best when they are artfully planted among green-leaved plants. Rather than placing individual gold-leaved plants among green ones, I plant groups or clusters to create a cohesive picture (see photo on p. 18). For example, in a border I might arrange gold-leaved plants from front to back, using varying heights, textures and forms. The proximity and variety allow the eye to travel smoothly across the border rather than stop abruptly at individual yellow plants. Then I echo their color with yellow-flowered plants (see photo on p. 16).

A rich backdrop of green effectively sets off a collection of gold-leaved

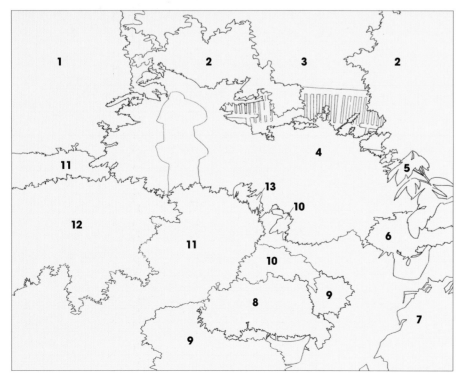

A composition in gold: Plants with golden leaves mingle beautifully with low-growing green shrubs. This golden garden is set off by a deep-green hedge of tall arborvitae.

Key to planting above

1. **Arborvitae**
   (*Thuja occidentalis* 'Hetz's Wintergreen')
2. **Mock orange**
   (*Philadelphus coronarius* 'Aureus')
3. **Hemlock**
   (*Tsuga canadensis*)
4. *Forsythia* x *intermedia* 'Gold Leaf'
5. **Bottlebrush buckeye**
   (*Aesculus parviflora*)
6. *Lantana camara* 'Lemon Swirl'
7. *Corylus avellana* 'Contorta'
8. **Feverfew**
   (*Chrysanthemum parthenium* 'Aureum')
9. *Vinca minor* 'Alba'
10. **Lungwort**
    (*Pulmonaria saccharata*)
11. *Daphne caucasica*
12. *Spiraea* x *bumalda* 'Gold Mound'
13. **Golden variegated hakone grass**
    (*Hakonechloa macra* 'Aureola')

Photo: Gary Mottau

SOURCES

Gold-leaved plants described by the author are offered by these sources.

Forestfarm, 990 Tetherow Road, Williams, OR 97544. Catalog, $3.

Heronswood Nursery, 7530 288th St. N.E., Kingston, WA 98346. Catalog, $3; minimum order, $25. Nursery open to visitors by appointment only.

Roslyn Nursery, 211 Burrs Lane, Dix Hills, NY 11746; 516-643-9347. Catalog, $3.

plants (see photo on p. 18). My best designs feature gold-leaved plants wrapped in hedges of arborvitae, hemlock or bottlebrush buckeye.

Siting plants correctly

To grow gold-leaved plants to perfection, you need to know how they perform in different sites. They are generally more sensitive to sun than their green-leaved counterparts. In too much sun, their leaves can scorch and turn brown. Excessive shade, however, can cause plants to lose color. For example, golden Japanese barberry (*Berberis thunbergii* `Aurea'*) has lime-green leaves in light shade, fades in full sun and reverts to green in full shade.

Other plants naturally change color as the season progresses, so they should be placed where they can be appreciated in spring. The golden hop vine (*Humulus lupulus* `Aureus'*) is such a plant (see photo at right). The foliage of this vine turns from light yellow-green to green.

Some gold-leaved plants that do well in the full sun of Northern regions will fry in the heat of a Southern sun. They may need the protection of midday shade when grown in the South—talk to a local gardener or nurseryperson who has tried them.

Many gold-leaved plants are available from mail-order nurseries (see Sources, above). I encourage you to experiment with foliage color, for the discovery of new combinations is part of the thrill of gardening. ☐

Gary Koller is a plantsperson, garden designer and instructor of landscape architecture at Harvard University's Graduate School of Design in Boston, Massachusetts.

Intensified by its setting: A yellow-green golden hop vine glows against a brick wall.

Hardy gold-leaved plants for the garden

Plant type	Plant name	Foliage color	Comments
Tree	**Golden black locust** (*Robinia pseudoacacia* `Frisia')	Yellow-green	30 ft. to 50 ft. tall; drought tolerant; needs sun
Shrub	**Golden Japanese Barberry** (*Berberis thunbergii* `Aurea')	Lime green	3 ft. to 4 ft. tall; drought tolerant; protect from hot sun
Shrub	**Gold-leaved forsythia** (*Forsythia x intermedia* `Gold Leaf')	Yellow	3 ft. to 5 ft. tall; needs light shade; yellow flowers in spring
Grass	**Golden variegated hakone grass** (*Hakonechloa macra* `Aureola')	Striped yellow/green	12 in. to 15 in. tall; protect from hot sun; prefers moist soil
Perennial	**Variegated yellow flag** (*Iris pseudacorus* `Variegata')	Pale yellow/green striped; turns green in summer	2 ft. to 3 ft. tall; prefers sun; gold flowers in summer
Vine	**Golden hop vine** (*Humulus lupulus* `Aureus')	Yellow-green; turns green in summer	20 ft. to 40 ft. tall; prefers sun; rampant grower; cut to ground in winter

The arching, grass-like leaves of a variegated sedge, *Carex × elata* 'Bowles Golden', light a shady garden corner with a golden glow. Edged with green, they contrast with the wide, green leaves, edged in gold, of the hosta in the background.

Leaves that Light Up the Garden

Shades of yellow, green and white provide color all season

by Tony Avent

Variegated plants enliven the garden. The stripes, spots and broad strokes of color that brighten their leaves add a welcome variety to the landscape. Flowers come and go, but the foliage of variegated plants provides constant interest, relieving the usual vista of green foliage with a range of colors, including white, cream, yellow, gold, pale green, purple and even pink. They also catch the eye with their patterns of variegation, sometimes bold, sometimes subtle and elegant. Instead of blurring into a wash of green, the leaves of a variegated plant stand out.

Variegated plants have several uses. Some can be used as the center of attention, a focal point in the landscape. Others provide bright foils for neighboring plants, or make a bridge between plants of competing colors and textures. Most variegated plants show off best against a dark background, and variegated trees and shrubs need larger trees or a mostly green hedge behind them to look their best.

The bold, central stripe and spiky leaves of *Yucca* 'Golden Sword' contrast beautifully with a bed of lantana and a backdrop of zinnias. Even when its flowers have come and gone, the yucca remains a center of attention, largely because of its green and gold variegation. Variegated leaves offer constant interest in the garden.

Variegated plants offer a trove of choices—there are variegated forms in more than 100 plant families and variegated forms of every kind of ornamental from ground covers to trees. Many of them are proven performers, readily available from garden centers and mail-order nurseries. Others are so unusual or so slow to grow that they will be relegated forever to the status of collector plants. If everyone else has the green form of plant X, then the plant collector wants the variegated form, often simply to be different. I value these plants—some for their beauty, but most of them for their rarity. I relish the challenge of blending them into my garden in Raleigh, North Carolina.

If you're new to variegated plants, you're likely to fall for some kinds of variegation more readily than for others. Leaves with neat edges of white or gold tend to be the most welcome in gardens. Leaves with variegated centers are also striking and fairly common. But you may find it hard at first to like plants streaked with uneven patterning and more than one color. Such plants are often prized by collectors and shunned by other gardeners, who think the plants just look diseased or mineral-deficient. Uneven patterns can be beautiful, if you give them a chance. You might start with the hosta (photo on p. 23).

Finding all of the plants I'm recommending is an adventure. Because there are variegated cultivars of trees, shrubs, grasses, annuals and herbaceous perennials, no single mail-order nursery carries all of them. Many will carry some, from just a few to as many as a few dozen. "Variegata" and "marginata" are two words to look for as you read catalogs this winter. It's worth the effort to search out my favorites, or similar ones.

What is variegation?

Variegation occurs when some normally green portion of a leaf lacks chlorophyll and so turns white, cream, yellow, or another color. There are several causes of variegation. It may first appear as a sport—a mutated sprout or branch on a normal plant. Occasionally, variegation is caused by a virus infection. Often, it is a genetic change, but one that is not passed reliably to seed-grown offspring, so new plants must be propagated by cuttings or division. (A nasturtium, *Tropaeolum* 'Alaska', is one of the few variegated plants that can be grown from seed.) Even when propagated and grown properly, many variegated plants have a tendency to revert and grow like their original,

Two variegated plants make eye-catching accents in the corner of a mixed border. The shrub is a dogwood, *Cornus alba* 'Elegantissima'. The wildly variegated leaves and vivid flowers belong to the nasturtium *Tropaeolum* 'Alaska', unusual among variegated plants because it is grown from seeds.

more vigorous, parents. In your garden, if a solid green branch or shoot appears on a variegated plant, just remove it immediately in order to retain the integrity of the variegation.

Variegated plants are less vigorous than their all-green cousins. Because they have less chlorophyll, they photosynthesize less and produce and store less energy. But most of them are, nonetheless, reliable garden plants. A few variegated plants tend to suffer more insect damage on the lighter parts of the foliage than in the green areas, due to the weaker tissue, but this is not true of all variegated plants and varies tremendously from species to species. Some variegated shrubs have also proved somewhat less cold-hardy than their all-green brethren. I'll recommend plants you can rely on, but experiment on your own, too. The rewards of variegation far outweigh its risks.

Shrubs to conifers

Shrubs are the most widely grown of variegated plants because they're so useful in the garden. The backbone of many gardens is the euonymus, of which variegated forms abound. My favorite of the upright forms remains *Euonymus japonica* 'Silver King', a shrub with beautiful, dark green leaves edged broadly in creamy white. It makes a great vertical accent in the garden.

There are also spreading kinds of euonymus that are used as ground covers. *Euonymus* 'Emerald 'n Gold' (green and yellow variegation), and 'Emerald Gaiety' (white and gold variegation) are two favorites for many areas of the country. They make large mats of evergreen color.

Variegated conifers are rare but choice. The most popular is the dragon's eye pine (*Pinus densiflora* 'Oculus-draconis'). It makes a spectacular sight with its horizontal banding of yellow and green. The false cypress family offers *Chamaecyparis pisifera* 'Snow', a dwarf with light green foliage tipped with white. In the South, the light color of the tips burns easily, so the plant must be grown in partial shade. A slow-growing conifer from Japan, *Cryptomeria japonica* 'Albospica' has a very similar appearance with a nice dusting of white over the branches.

Not to be outdone is arborvitae, the backbone of the garden conifers. *Thuja occidentalis* 'Sherwood Frost' is a beautiful, slow-growing cultivar with a dusting of white that becomes more prevalent in late summer and fall. One of my favorites, *T. plicata* 'Zebrina', has stunning variegation of gold and green, but unfortunately it does not color well in our heat. Perhaps in the Pacific Northwest and in more northerly climates this cultivar would be highly prized.

Bright yellow and edged with green, the leaves of *Sedum × alboroseum* 'Medio-variegatus' contrast strikingly with the tall blue spikes of *Salvia* 'Blue Queen'. The soft pink flowers of *Lychnis coronaria* 'Angel Blush' frame the combination.

Dogwoods that gleam

The dogwood family boasts many variegated members. One of my favorites is the giant variegated dogwood, *Cornus controversa* 'Variegata'. The variegation is a good, wide, clean white edge contrasted against the dark green leaf center and the nearly black stems. (For more details on this dogwood, see *FG* #28, p. 18.)

Smaller tree and shrub forms of variegated dogwood are more widely available. Our native flowering dogwood, *C. florida*, has yielded many selections, such as 'Cherokee Daybreak', with white variegation and white flowers; 'Cherokee Sunset', with yellow variegation and pink flowers; and 'First Lady', with yellow variegation and white flowers, to mention just a few. Two great selections of the kousa dogwood, *(C. kousa)* are also available. 'Snowboy' has spectacular white-edged foliage, which looks as though each leaf is hand-painted. My personal favorite is 'Gold Star', which has been on my

VARIEGATED HOSTAS STAR IN THE SHADE

Hostas are the variegated royalty of the shade garden. They offer an exceptional variety of yellow, white and light green markings to brighten shady spots. In the popularity poll of the *American Hosta Society*, eight of the top ten hostas are variegated.

The most common variegated hosta, *Hosta undulata*, has been grown by nearly everyone who has ever grown any hostas—it's the mostly white one with green edges. It grows vigorously and is tough as nails. Unfortunately, the poor leaf substance and horrendously ugly flowers make this cultivar one of the worst choices for a garden.

Among the older cultivars, *Hosta* 'Francee' and *Hosta* 'Antioch' rank with the finest of all variegated hostas. 'Francee' has wide leaves of deep green, with a thin white margin. It eventually becomes quite large, with a spread of 4 ft. 'Antioch' emerges in the spring with a light green leaf edged in yellow. As the season progresses, the edge changes into a lovely, creamy white. One clump of 'Antioch', with its 5-ft. spread, can transform a dark garden.

One of the best and newest variegated hostas is the strikingly beautiful 'Great Expectations', which emerges with a yellow center that gradually turns to creamy white. Since the lack of chlorophyll in the main portion of the leaf allows less tissue to produce food, the white-centered hostas are usually more difficult to grow. 'Great Expectations' is one of the few white-centered hostas that actually grow well, especially when it's planted in partial sun.

A species with an array of variegations is *H. montana*. The cultivar 'Aureo marginata' is always a popular favorite even though it emerges early, is subject to late frosts and is often burned back by hot summer weather. The green-centered leaf is edged in a vivid yellow band. 'Mountain Snow' has the same green center and a nice white edge, and 'On Stage' (which prefers morning sun), has a spectacular yellow center and a green edge, a combination which is sure to catch everyone's eye.

One of the oldest variegated cultivars is *Hosta* 'Frances Williams'. This large, blue-leaved hosta has a wide, yellow edge, and it is still quite popular, although the yellow edge is less tolerant of adverse weather conditions than the green center and often tends to burn. The hosta world is currently full of 'Frances Williams' look-alikes that reportedly have solved this problem, but no clear favorite has emerged to replace this very popular variety.

Another attribute of some variegated hostas is fragrant blooms, thanks to breeding efforts in the last decade. 'Sugar and Cream', 'Iron Gate Glamour', 'Summer Fragrance', and 'So Sweet' are all worth growing. The best of the scented variegated hostas so far, however, is 'Fragrant Bouquet'. This lime-green-centered hosta has a white edge and masses of very fragrant, white flowers. Be sure to plant this one where it can be enjoyed often.

Although they are eye-catching in themselves, variegated hostas can be combined effectively with other shade plants. They can contrast with the lacy fronds of ferns or can echo the colors of solid blue, gold or green hostas. If you use several different variegated hostas in one area, separate them with other types of plants. Otherwise, the garden may look jumbled, and the beauty of the individual leaf patterns can be lost.

—T.A.

The yellow-centered leaves of *Hosta* 'On Stage' are outlined and washed with delicate shades of green and chartreuse. 'On Stage' shows its richest variegations when grown in partial sun, and fades to more yellow if grown in all shade.

lust list since I saw a spectacular specimen in South Carolina. (See photo on p. 25.) 'Gold Star' has a wide, creamy yellow band through the center of each leaf. Although some specimens seem to revert, others appear completely stable.

Among bush dogwoods there are wonderful variegations. *C. alba* 'Elegantissima', which has red stems and green leaves with a white edge, is the most popular. *C. sericea* 'Silver and Gold' has the same leaf pattern, but with yellow stems. *C. alba* 'Gouchaultii', a less familiar cultivar, has yellow leaf margins and red stems. Bush dogwoods grow well in the coldest parts of the continental U.S., but they don't perform well in the Deep South.

There is one last decid-uous shrub I can recommend enthusiastically. The few available variegated cultivars of forsythia have been poor performers, at least in the South, until now, with the arrival of *Forsythia* 'Fiesta' from New Zealand. A dwarf (3 ft. by 3 ft.), it has beautiful gold foliage with a stable green edge. It is still unknown in American gardens, but some nurseries are propagating it for eventual sale.

Striped grasses

Ornamental grasses are a personal favorite for a sunny spot in the garden. From USDA Hardiness Zone 5 (-20°F) southward, folks are gradually learning about the variegated miscanthus. The most common is *Miscanthus sinensis* 'Variegatus', a relatively large, clumping grass with dynamic vertical striping, which gives it an almost-white appearance from a distance. The biggest breakthrough for smaller gardens is *M. sinensis* 'Morning Light'. The variegation on this grass is so subtle, and the texture so delicate, that even those who hate variegated plants would fall in love with 'Morning Light'.

There are several miscanthus cultivars with horizontal bands, the most unusual type of variegation. *M. sinensis* 'Zebrinus' forms a large, spreading clump, while *M. sinensis* 'Strictus' is a very upright selection with heavier stripes. A new selection from North Carolina is *M. sinensis* 'Kirk Alexander'. While it's not as heavily striped, its dwarf stature and wonderful plumage make it a hit with the owners of small gardens.

Sedges resemble grasses, but prefer to grow in partly shaded spots. The most widely available variegated sedge is *Carex hachijoensis* 'Evergold' (or 'Old Gold'). This striped, weeping sedge is perfect planted beside a pond, which will reflect its

Horizontal bands of gold paint the 5 ft. blades of a mature porcupine grass, *Miscanthus sinensis* 'Strictus', that shares a border with yellow daylilies and lavender-blue Russian sage. Horizontal striping is the rarest pattern of variegation.

weeping foliage. *C. morrowii temnolepis* is very similar in stature, but has a finer texture and a silvery cast.

For a border, no sedge is better than *C. conica* 'Marginata', a spectacular white sedge edged in green. If only it were better known in the trade, I'm convinced it would replace liriope, which it resembles. Two cultivars of *C. morrowii*, 'Variegata' and 'Gilt Edge', make wonderful clumps with age. Their upright growth provides a good contrast with mounding foliage.

Yes, perennials too

Perennials are the easiest of variegated plants to work with in the garden. Because of their size, they can be plugged into the landscape easily to provide an accent or a touch of color as needed. For a sunny garden from Zone 4 (-30°F) southward, variegated yuccas can be ideal. Both *Yucca smalliana* 'Bright Edge' (green with a yellow edge) and *Y. filamentosa* 'Golden Sword' (green with gold center) are quite handsome in the sunny garden. (See photo on p. 21.) My personal favorite is *Y. filamentosa* 'Variegata'. This medium-size yucca has wide, ivory-white edges that make it one of the most eye-catching plants in the garden, especially when its towering spikes of white flowers are in bloom.

Among my favorite variegated perennials for sun are the sedums, primarily *Sedum lineare* 'Variegatum', a low-growing, needle-leaf type with green leaves and a nice white edge. For something bolder, you might try *Sedum × alboroseum* 'Mediovariegatus'. A bright gold sedum with a green edge, it is a great accent against darker colors such as blues.

A favorite for shade

There are many wonderful variegated perennials for shade, including the likes of ajuga, Solomon's seal, pulmonaria, ferns, lamium and hosta. (There are so many variegated hostas that I've grouped them separately on p. 23.) My favorite is the variegated Solomon's seal, *Polygonatum odoratum* 'Variegatum'. This perennial grows seemingly anywhere and never too fast or too slow. The arching stems of green foliage edged in white carry tiny, dangling white flowers in spring. Variegated Solomon's seal seems capable of complementing almost everything, from dark blue hostas to nearly any type of fern.

Lamiums are a good ground cover in shade. To lighten the woodland floor, try *Lamium maculatum* 'Beacon Silver' (silver center and purple flowers), *L. maculatum* 'Pink Pewter' (silver center and pink flowers), and *L. maculatum* 'White Nancy' (silver center and white flowers). The lamiums all grow to nearly 12 in. tall and spread to nearly 4 ft. in width. Lamiums should not be planted around tiny woodland plants because they could overrun them.

One fern stands out as the variegated leader for most parts of the country. Japanese painted fern, *Athyrium nipponicum* 'Pic-

A bold stroke of yellow brightens a leaf of the kousa dogwood 'Gold Star'. The variegation provides color in the landscape long after the spring flowers have faded.

tum', is a striking addition to the shade garden. Although it varies tremendously when grown from spores, the characteristic purple, gray and green variegation can be standardized by dividing the clumps. Another wonderful, but lesser-known, variegated fern is *A. otophorum*. The variegation is similar to that of *A. nipponicum*, but this fern has a more open and stately habit.

I hope you are ready to try variegated plants in your garden. Use variegation as a design tool, highlighting the chosen plant and complementing its neighbors. With careful placement that integrates both the texture and the color, variegated plants can be an essential element of the garden. □

Tony Avent has his own botanical garden and mail-order nursery at his home in Raleigh, North Carolina.

A clump of variegated Solomon's seal (*Polygonatum odoratum* 'Variegatum') shows off bright green leaves edged with a delicate stroke of white. A shade-tolerant perennial, Solomon's seal spreads gradually in a non-aggressive way, and the variegated form brightens dark corners.

Photos: top, Mark Kane: right, Susan Kahn

Big, Bold Yellows
Sunny flowers fill the summer garden

The 10-in. blooms of 'Taiyo' sunflower add a bold, glowing accent to the late-summer garden. Like the other large, yellow-flowered plants grown by the author, 'Taiyo' demands very little care.

by Alice Yarborough

Gardeners have always treasured big, imposing plants. Wordsworth may have praised "a violet by a mossy stone, half hidden from the eye," and catalogs may advertise a large assortment of compact cultivars, but tall plants dispense a special joy. Gardens need a few whopping big plants to break the monotony of the small.

In my own modest-sized garden, I escape boredom by using six big plants that boast two other attractions—brilliant yellow flowers and large, striking leaves. In my flower beds and borders, these big, bold yellows are accent plants, but in groups, most could also serve as an attractive seasonal hedge or screen. All are of very easy culture—they don't need fertilizing or mulching, they aren't prone to diseases, most pests ignore them, and, despite their size, they're not invasive. My garden is near Seattle, Washington, in USDA Hardiness Zone 7 (0°F), but most of these beauties can be grown in a wide geographical range.

Olympic mullein

The soft yellow flower spires of Olympic mullein (*Verbascum olympicum*) tower 8 ft. to 12 ft. above a large basal rosette of hairy, gray-green leaves. New blossoms open each morning, giving the plant a fresh look every day. This mullein blooms throughout the summer, beginning in June of its second year. All summer long, honeybees and bumblebees browse its lemon-scented flowers, stuffing their pollen baskets.

Hardy to Zone 5 (-20°F) or 6 (-10°F), Olympic mullein holds its leaves through the winter. Some of my plants may be biennial hybrids of the perennial Olympic mullein, but a few behave as true perennials and occasionally live on to bloom for three or four years. In any case, Olympic mullein is lovely, and I start a few seedlings every year to insure I'll never be without it.

Olympic mullein is indispensable in my garden. Although this plant can soar to an imposing height, its cheerful informality suggests an old-fashioned garden to me. I use these stately plants as single specimens, or I group two or three together. If I'm growing several plants, I space them 18 in.

The long, yellow flower spires of Olympic mullein (above) light up the author's perennial garden. The fringed flowers and fragrant stems of scented oxeye (below) give pleasure to the nose and eye.

to 20 in. apart, so their leaf rosettes ultimately overlap.

I grow my plants in full sun, though the flowers wilt a trifle on hot summer afternoons. Olympic mullein prefers lean soils, but handles rich, heavy ones better than do most other mulleins. The plants are drought-resistant, but to produce a showier plant, I water mine thoroughly about every ten days in the summer. Good drainage is essential, however, as mulleins will rot in soggy ground.

I remove the central flower stalk once it has finished blooming in order to spur already-blossoming side shoots to flower more. To encourage production of new, leafy basal shoots, I also cut back the entire plant to the ground in late August. I do occasionally need to stake it, especially when a ten-foot plant starts to list drunkenly to one side.

I grow Olympic mullein from seeds, but you can also order plants by mail (see 1,3,4 in Sources on p. 29; the numbers are keyed to nurseries and seed companies). I sow seeds in June. If I sow earlier, the plants sometimes bloom in late October, only to be struck by frost and then diminished in vigor the next summer. I also grow volunteers, seedlings which appear in the garden each year.

Scented oxeye

Scented oxeye (*Telekia speciosa*) bears clusters of golden daisies held above heart-shaped leaves measuring more than 1 ft. long. The finely wrought, twisted rays of the elegant flowers bring to mind the work of a medieval goldsmith. As the flower heads age, their central yellow discs turn attractively fuzzy and brown. The lightest touch of this plant's fragrant stems leaves a strongly aromatic scent on your fingers.

An herbaceous perennial, 5½ ft. tall with equal spread, scented oxeye is hardy to Zone 3 (-40°F). It blooms in my garden throughout June and into July, beginning in its second year.

Because its large leaves are attractive both before and after bloom, scented oxeye need not be relegated to the back of the border. An upfront

Caucasian inula (above), a vigorously growing perennial, flourishes in sun or part shade, and in a wide range of soils. Rising above 9-in. wide, heart-shaped leaves, the yellow flowers of ligularia 'The Rocket' (below) serve as bright sentinels alongside a house.

position allows close inspection of the flowers and the many butterflies they attract. A single, established plant will attain shrub-like proportions in one summer. Three or four plants, spaced 5 ft. apart, make a gleaming seasonal hedge.

Although quite tolerant of poor soils, scented oxeye requires ample moisture. My plant thrives in full sun, but would do fine in partial shade. In late fall, after its leaves have yellowed, I cut my oxeye back to the ground.

You can start oxeye from seeds (available from 1,3; some catalogs list it as *Buphthalum speciosum*). Sow seeds indoors or directly in the garden in late April or early May. You can also propagate scented oxeye by dividing it, but division doesn't seem to be required. Plants will self-sow if you don't remove spent blossoms.

Caucasian inula

An herbaceous perennial, Caucasian inula (*Inula magnifica*), rises to 8 ft. tall with a 5-ft. spread. Its spidery, 6-in. wide, yellow daisy flowers grow in clusters above its enormous, deep green leaves, some of them up to 1 yd. long. Hardy to Zone 3, this

beauty flowers from mid-June through July, beginning in its second year.

My inula grows at the rear of the garden in the shade of a big black locust tree. Its yellow daisies light up an area where few other flowers would

thrive. A background position is wise, as inula's big leaves get a bit ratty-looking after it blooms.

Caucasian inula performs well in full sun or in considerable shade. It prospers in rich or poor soils, and up to a point, tolerates boggy ones. In fact, inula is a moisture-lover, so I make sure the soil around it never dries out. In the spring, I bait for slugs, which otherwise would eat the leaves; in early August, I deadhead my plants, and in late fall I cut back the stalks close to ground level.

I started my plants from seeds (available from 1) sown in the garden in July, but you could plant earlier. Caucasian inula grows so robustly that just one seedling will produce a large clump by its third year. In my garden, I spaced several seedlings 10 in. apart to produce a clump sooner.

Don't be alarmed when your inula seedlings die down in the fall. Come spring, you'll see new shoots popping up. I put plant markers by the seedlings before they die down so I can distinguish them from the weeds. You can divide inula in early spring, but it's not necessary.

Ligularia stenocephala 'The Rocket'

'The Rocket' has gorgeous heart-shaped, toothed leaves, up to 9-in. across. Spires of small, yellow flowers stud its wiry, 5-ft. tall, black stems. This herbaceous perennial, hardy to Zone 5, blooms in my area in late June throughout July, beginning in its second summer.

Grow 'The Rocket' where its elegant leaves won't be concealed behind other plants. An upfront position will also let you sniff the sweet fragrance of its flowers. Space plants 3 ft. apart.

'The Rocket' is a plant with peculiar habits. It requires some light to bloom well, but when hot sunshine hits its big, lovely leaves, they wilt dramatically, however moist the soil, and look quite horrid. Fortunately, when afternoon shade arrives, the plant speedily perks up and looks gorgeous again. In my garden, 'The Rocket' grows in a bed that receives a few hours of mid-morning sun—enough to encourage plenty of flowers while minimizing wilting. 'The Rocket' does best in a rich, humusy soil that holds moisture well. In hot weather, I water it every other day.

I started with plants of 'The Rocket' (available from 4,5,6,7). Seeds are available only for the species, which is almost as showy as 'The Rocket'

Photos these two pages: Alice Yarborough

and requires identical culture. You can also propagate plants by dividing them in the spring.

Despite its height, this ligularia doesn't require staking. In late fall, I cut my plants back close to the ground. Slugs love their big, soft leaves, so I set out bait and don't mulch the plants (mulch provides the slugs with hiding places). The only insect pests have been a few spittlebugs, which I pick off by hand.

Globe centaurea

Globe centaurea (*Centaurea macrocephala*), bears uninspiring, coarse leaves, but its brilliant yellow, thistle-like blossoms are magnificent. Its bloom period is short, yet its showy flowers and easy-care nature should make gardeners forgiving of the brevity of its display. For several weeks in midsummer, the flowers attract butterflies, bumblebees and humans. Shiny, light brown bracts surround the flowers, adding considerably to their beauty. I usually position globe centaurea among later-blooming plants, such as chrysanthemums, which provide color when the centaurea's show is over. Hardy to Zone 3, these herbaceous perennials reach 4 ft. tall with a 3-ft. spread.

Given adequate drainage, full sun and an occasional swig of water, globe centaurea does well in most soils. It never needs staking and isn't troubled by pests or diseases.

Globe centaurea seeds and plants are readily available (from 1,2,3,5,6,7). The plants are very easy to grow from seeds started indoors or sown directly in the garden in mid-spring. Space or thin plants to 2½ ft. to 3 ft. apart. Globe centaurea grows rapidly, but won't bloom until its second year. I divide my plants every fourth or fifth year in early spring or fall.

'Taiyo' sunflower

Just looking at the cheerful faces of 'Taiyo' sunflowers brightens a misty September morning. As beguiling as taller sunflowers, this 5½ ft. tall cultivar, *Helianthus annuus* 'Taiyo', holds its 10-in. wide flower head up much better and never needs staking. A hardy annual, 'Taiyo' blooms in my garden from early August well into September. Its wide, nectar-laden flower heads are so attractive to bees and butterflies that I often think of them as dinner plates.

Some years I grow 'Taiyo' in a flower border, other times in a corner of a vegetable patch. While mammoth

In midsummer, many thistle-like flowers are sprinkled among the deep green leaves of globe centaurea.

SOURCES

The following mail-order sources carry seeds or plants of at least two of the plants described in this article.

Seeds:

1. J.L. Hudson, Seedsman, P.O. Box 1058, Redwood City, CA 94064. Catalog $1.

2. Park Seed Co., Cokesbury Road, Greenwood, SC 29647-0001, 803-223-7333. Catalog free.

3. Thompson and Morgan Inc., P.O. Box 11308, Jackson, NJ 08527, 908-363-2225. Catalog free.

Plants:

4. Kurt Bluemel, Inc., 2740 Greene Lane, Baldwin, MD 21013-9523, 301-557-7229. Catalog $3.

5. Carroll Gardens, 444 East Main St., P.O. Box 310, Westminster, MD 21157, 800-638-6334. Catalog $2, deductible from first order.

6. Forestfarm, 990 Tetherow Rd., Williams, OR 97544. Catalog $3.

7. Milaeger's Gardens, 4838 Douglas Ave., Racine, WI 53402. 414-639-2371. Catalog $1. Minimum order, $25 .

sunflowers seem inappropriate in the flower bed, the middle-sized 'Taiyo' fits in nicely. I usually group six or seven plants in a couple of staggered rows at the rear of the bed, sowing seeds (available from 1,2) 14 in. to 16 in. apart in early May. Planted 1 ft. apart, fast-growing 'Taiyo' plants can also serve as a seasonal hedge.

'Taiyo' requires full sun and does nicely in average soils. I give my plants a deep watering weekly, and I bait for slugs. Unlike its giant relatives, 'Taiyo' can produce good-sized flower heads on side shoots. After the large central flower head has faded, I cut it off at the base, and secondary flower heads quickly develop.

Families of deer mice eagerly await my annual, early May sowing of sunflower seeds, which they exhume and devour. Any seeds they have overlooked will sprout—only to become mouse salad greens. This past year I outwitted the mice by capping each planted seed with an inverted plastic mesh basket of the kind used to package supermarket berries. I left the baskets in place until the seedlings had grown several sets of leaves. After that the mouse gourmets left them alone. Later, in the fall, hungry jays harvest the developing seed meats, which are really too small for human consumption anyway.

Once I carried a single 'Taiyo' sunflower to a very old, sick lady in a Seattle hospital. It was a surprising experience. Strangers on the bus, on city sidewalks, in hospital corridors, smiled and paused to pay their tributes to the blossom. It seems there's just something about a sunflower.... □

Alice Yarborough gardens in Carnation, Washington.

Spring Whites
Highlights in a small urban garden

by Betty Gatewood

I got the idea for my white spring garden almost accidentally. A pear tree overhanging my yard burst into a cloud of white just as some intensely red tulips I had planted in a bed beneath it began to color. By the time the tulips were in full bloom, the pear tree had shed a million white petals over my flower bed. The fallen petals were lovely; I found I liked them more than my own tulips. Another neighbor's planting of tall white tulips against dark evergreens gave me further inspiration. So I planted two clumps of white 'Carrara' tulips and the following spring was delighted with the results.

At first, my idea was to use white and a few pale colors only—as nature does in the Northeast, where spring wildflowers are mostly white and pink. Although I've come up with combinations of pale colors that I've liked very much, I find that my spring garden gets whiter every year. Since my summer-blooming perennials are about as gaudy as vegetation can get, I find the understated spring colors a welcome contrast.

My house, in Ossining, a Hudson River village 30 miles north of New York City, is on a narrow site, 50 ft. wide by 165 ft. deep. There's a small front yard, but the most gardenable space is the rectangular backyard, which is made even narrower by a long driveway to a garage near the back of the lot. As my main gardening interest is in growing perennials in mixed borders, I've squeezed a lot of flower bed from my small backyard. I started with one 40-ft.-long border, but after garden mania set in I put in a second, which has now swallowed up much of the lawn. Other plantings are tucked in at the edges of the long driveway and against the foundation of the house. The garden has thus grown by accretion, and the more or less proper plan I started out with has succumbed to an enthusiasm for plants.

Because I don't have the space to make a separate spring garden with

The large feathery blossoms of this parrot tulip sit atop sturdy stalks in this three-year-old planting.

Gatewood's favorite white daffodil is 'Thalia', which grows to about 12 in. in height.

masses of tulips, banks of azaleas and so on, I've put in spring plants—bulbs, perennials and shrubs—wherever I could find room. The white flowers show up well above the leaves of the summer-blooming perennials, and the perennials' leaves later conceal the bulbs' fading foliage. Best of all, the garden looks completely different in spring and summer. It's almost as good as having twice as much garden.

From the beginning, I decided to seek out old-fashioned and even "ordinary"

white plants. I've frequently found that the common plants that are readily available and inexpensive are the most satisfying in the long run. (I've bought most of the plants listed in this article at local nurseries or from familiar mail-order catalogs; I've given sources for those I've had more difficulty finding.) Most often I merely choose the plants I like. Occasionally I try to find something specifically short, tall, shade-loving or tough, but most of my effort has gone into simply achieving a continuous sequence of bloom from plants that I like. Usually I try to plan plant combinations, but many of my happiest combinations have happened by accident, the result of my having to find a place for some plant I couldn't pass up.

Bulbs

Snowdrops (*Galanthus nivalis*) are the first white blooms in my garden, but they are an embarrassingly meager show. Over the years I've planted several hundred snowdrop bulbs in what seemed to be likely sites around the yard. But I've never had more than a dozen blooms, each in woeful isolation from its neighbors—and few things look as sad as a lone snowdrop. I'm beginning to conclude that the common advice to start snowdrops by lifting a division from an existing colony must have some merit to it.

To console myself for the lack of snowdrops, I've sprinkled several varieties of white crocuses in the lawn where I can see them from the house. My favorite, the small 'Snow Bunting' (*Crocus chrysanthus*), is just beginning to establish itself near a colony of deep-blue chionodoxas, the legacy of a previous gardener at this site. Both plantings bloom at about the same time and make an attractive combination. (I got my 'Snow Bunting' from McClure & Zimmerman, 108 W. Winnebago, P.O. Box 368, Friesland, WI 53935.)

A satisfactory spring garden certainly requires daffodils. Of the white daffodils available—from pure whites to creams to whites with variously colored trumpets—I've stuck with the plainest and whitest. My first daffodils, 50 bulbs of 'Mt. Hood', an old and widely available early large-trumpet type, were a disappointment. The catalog photographs typically show a pure-white flower, but I discovered that when 'Mt. Hood' opens, its trumpet is distinctly yellow, and it doesn't fade to white for several days. Since daffodils bloom in staggered fashion, my planting of 'Mt. Hood' always has a motley appearance. (In a planting based on white and yellow, of course, this would be fine.)

Fortunately, I've found several other narcissus that I like better than 'Mt. Hood'. My favorite without question is 'Thalia' (bottom photo, facing page), which opens with a faint hint of ivory and quickly fades to pure white. It is a moderately late variety, coming into bloom in my coolish site around April 20, just preceding the bloom of the white-flowering dogwood it's planted beneath. Less exotic-looking than 'Thalia', and earlier, is 'Beersheba', a creamy-white trumpet that has done well for me. To my eye, 'Beersheba' has a more elegant shape than does 'Mt. Hood', but best of all it's not half yellow when it opens. (McClure & Zimmerman offers Beersheba also.)

I like two other white narcissus very much. 'Actaea', the poet's narcissus, is pure white with a yellow eye rimmed with red (top photo at right). This sounds something like a narcissus with a hangover—and it looks garish enough in some photographs that I put off planting it for several years. But it looks fine in the garden. A few dozen 'Actaea' planted in the border opposite my old bank of 'King Alfred' finally convinced me to exile the king for good. The only drawback to 'Actaea' is its grassy, floppy foliage, which is more unsightly than that of most daffodils. I usually interplant it with annuals (cornflowers, calendulas) to hide the leaves during early summer. 'Actaea' is also late; it peaks for me around the first week in May.

Even later is the oddly named 'Geranium', which I grow primarily for cutting. It looks something like its relative, the paper-white narcissus, but has a vivid-orange cup. I don't love the orange, but I do love this cultivar's strong, sweet scent, as pungent as that of the late summer lilies. This and its generous bloom (as many as five flowers per stalk) make it a great cut flower, one that arranges itself in a vase and perfumes a room pleasantly.

By the time the narcissus are waning, I have several kinds of white tulips in bloom. The first—and my favorite—is 'White Parrot', a 20-in.-tall tulip that peaks for me around May 1, early for a parrot type (top photo, facing page). It is a very large-flowered tulip, but a well-proportioned one. I think most parrot tulips are too cabbagey or wildly colored to look attractive

A spray of Thunberg spirea trails through 'Actaea' daffodils (top), two of the white spring-flowering plants in Gatewood's garden. The spirea's profuse bloom anchors the end of a border (bottom).

Photos this page: Staff

Sprinkling small clumps of tulips throughout the border gives a springtime feeling and adds interest to areas that fill in later in the season. The white tulips in the foreground are 'Carrara'; in the background is the white tulip 'Maureen'. The pink tulips are 'Pink Diamond' and 'Esther'.

The pure-white stars of 'Clusiana', a small species tulip, stand out in a shady spot, above a bed of sweet woodruff.

Candytuft spills over an otherwise nondescript retaining wall in Gatewood's narrow side yard.

in the garden, but 'White Parrot' has a feathery, swanlike appearance. I've put two clumps of eight or so bulbs each between peonies in the border. They bloom when the peonies are still shoots; later the peonies conceal the spent tulips. Tulips often weaken after a year or two, but my three-year-old 'White Parrot' plantings are still blooming vigorously.

As for plain white tulips, an excellent (though very tall) one is 'Maureen'. Because of its extreme height, around 30 in., it needs company to avoid a bean-pole effect. I've planted it at the back of one border, where it stands out against a gray fence. 'Carrara', my first white tulip, is a more manageable height, around 24 in. (photo, above left). 'Carrara' also has a lovely shape—a perfect oval, like a hard-boiled egg on a stalk—but it takes on color very gradually. It needs more than a week to turn from green to yellow to cream, unlike 'Maureen' or 'White Parrot', which go from green to white in about two days. 'Alabaster' blooms about a week later than 'Maureen', and it goes from green to pure white in a flash. It's a good height, about 24 in., but its form is a little blocky and less elegant than that of 'Carrara'. I plant 'White Triumphator', the commonly available white lily-flowering tulip, where its tall (26-in.) but weak stem is protected from wind. I also need to plant new bulbs of it roughly every two years or it begins to decline.

Not all my white tulips are entirely white. The flowers of 'Clusiana', a small species tulip known as the candystick tulip, give the effect of pure-white stars when they open flat in the sun (photo,

above center). When they close, however, the red stripes on the outside show, but the redness is subtle and not out of keeping with a white effect. I planted some 'Clusiana' in a bed of sweet woodruff (*Galium odoratum*). They bloom simultaneously and the effect is very pleasing.

For several years, I planted tulips in large bunches, eight or ten together, following the common advice against scattering bulbs too thinly. Then, inspired by a border I saw on Cape Cod, I started dotting groups of three or five around the bed. This gives the impression that the entire border is in bloom, and later the smaller clumps of deteriorating leaves are much easier to hide.

Perennials

When I began my white plantings, half a dozen plants of candytuft (*Iberis sempervirens*) already inhabited some pockets of a rather ugly retaining wall. I liked them well enough to extend the planting. I've since tried the twice-blooming candytuft 'Autumn Snow' and I wish I'd planted it from the first (photo, above right). Not all plant suppliers have this variety, but it's worth seeking out if you want a second bloom in the fall. (I bought 'Autumn Snow' from Bluestone Perennials, 7211 Middle Ridge Rd., Madison, OH 44057.) Besides its abundant bloom, candytuft has the virtue of being evergreen and tough, although it does look fatigued in winter. The only special care I give it is a once-over shearing with kitchen scissors after bloom to keep it tidy; I cut it to about 3 in. to 4 in. high.

Sweet woodruff is one of my favorite

spring whites, and I seem to add more of it every year. My one attempt to grow it from seed was an utter rout, so I've settled for buying small plants. (I get them from Bluestone also.) It does spread, but is easy enough to pull. It's one of the most beautiful ground covers merely for its foliage, and though not evergreen it stays perky and attractive from mid-April till a fairly hard frost. One of my sweet-woodruff plantings points up a great virtue of white flowers: their ability to combine with flowers of other colors. Under a Japanese maple in the border, I have woodruff interspersed with English bluebells. Nearby are blue and white sweet William (*Phlox divaricata*) and two geraniums, 'Johnson's Blue' and 'Wargrave Pink'.

Three other white perennials—forget-me-nots, bleeding-hearts and trilliums—have done well for me in light shade. I've used white forget-me-nots (*Myosotis*) at the shady end of my borders at the feet of daffodils. I think the white form of bleeding-heart (*Dicentra spectabilis* 'Alba') has a delicacy that its red-and-white relative lacks. (White Flower Farm, Litchfield, CT 06759, carries 'Alba'.) Blooming about the same time as the bleeding-heart is *Trillium grandiflorum* (left photo, facing page), the familiar wildflower of the northeastern woods. I had thought it touchy to grow, but my initial six plants have expanded into a colony.

Shrubs

I have two white-flowering trees at one side of the house, a dogwood and a Bradford pear. Unfortunately, I don't have space for more trees, but I do have room

White trilliums (*Trillium grandiflorum*) nestle in Gatewood's one shady corner.

Star magnolia blooms early, before leafing out. It justifies its place in the garden year round — handsome leaves in the summer, attractive branches and bark in the winter.

Gatewood uses the icy-white blossoms of the azalea 'Delaware Valley White' as cut flowers.

for shrubs, which are an outstanding source of spring white in my garden. The first to bloom, around April 15, is a star magnolia, *Magnolia stellata,* which when full-grown is almost a small tree (photo, above center). Its charm, besides its lovely and slightly fragrant flowers, is its earliness of bloom. Like forsythia, its flowers emerge before the leaves, bursting from furry pods long before most other plants have leafed out. This shrub is also handsome in leaf, and even when leafless in winter; its trunk and branches are shapely and its bark light gray. I've had mine only two years and it's still blooming shyly, but already I'm pleased that I put it in a prominent site readily visible from the house.

Blooming after the star magnolia are two Thunberg spireas (*Spiraea Thunbergii*) planted at the end of the border, as shown on p. 31. (I got mine from White Flower Farm.) Why this spirea is not as widely planted as forsythia (or more so) is a mystery to me. It comes into bloom slowly, the tiny white flowers producing a kind of lacy or soapsudsy effect that grows gradually brighter until by the end of April the shrub is an absolute monster of white bloom. If this weren't enough, its small light-green linear leaves look delicate and fresh all summer, and turn a pleasant coral-orange in the fall. Many of the fine branches that flower die back, and I trim off these dead twigs with a scissors a month or so after the flowers have faded. This isn't compulsory, but it greatly improves the shrub's appearance and bloom the following year. The only other care required is to cultivate lightly to get rid of small, fragile seedlings that will

spring up in open soil beneath the plant.

My experience with the Thunberg spirea has been so positive that last spring I bought several more and made a hedge of them in my front yard. I've read that they'll grow to 5 ft. or so and can be trimmed to a boxy shape, but I think most of their charm comes from their swooping, swirling habit. Mine are 4 ft. tall and I intend to let them get as exuberant as they please.

I have two other spireas. I filled a space at the corner of my lot near the street with *Spiraea prunifolia,* the common bridal-wreath. It blooms just after the Thunberg, and about two weeks later comes *Spiraea × Vanhouttei* (sometimes called bridal-wreath as well). These shrubs were once common; both were in a garden I knew as a child. Nowadays they seem to have fallen out of fashion in favor of the flashier and more compact azaleas. But I like them very much, however old-fashioned and space-hogging they are. I think *S. × Vanhouttei* is the more appealing of the two; its blue-green leaves are more interesting and emerge attractively before the flowers. But there is something special about the flowers of *S. prunifolia,* each like a tiny old-fashioned white rose. I'd hate to have a garden without it, even though it is the rangiest grower of all and completely undistinguished (even a bit ratty) after it blooms. Fortunately, I barely see it through most of the year. By contrast, my *S. × Vanhouttei* is planted as a foundation plant alongside my front porch, and nothing could look more appropriate against white painted Victorian latticework.

I've found all these spireas extremely easy to grow. The Thunbergs thrive in full sun and good garden soil, and the others are doing fine in mediocre soil and some shade. All flowered as young plants and have since grown about 6 in. each year. Because *S. prunifolia* grows to about 9 ft. and *S. × Vanhouttei* to around 7 ft., I may eventually have to prune or move them.

Around May 15—between *S. prunifolia* and *S. × Vanhouttei*—my one white azalea blooms. 'Delaware Valley White' is officially an evergreen, but mine is neither very green nor very attractive in winter. Planted near a hemlock along with mountain laurel, tulips and sweet woodruff, it becomes more presentable in April and redeems itself in May (photo, above right). The blooms are pure icy white, and although most people don't use azaleas as a cut flower, I like to cut a few branches for a vase—they last well in water.

By the end of May, my garden starts to take on color. I have my first rose around May 25, blue bearded irises a few days later, and then a great spate of pink and white peonies. With that, the summer garden has begun. The whites don't entirely stop. There are white climbing roses, white phlox and so on until the Japanese anemones and the last white chrysanthemums bring my gardening year to a close. Then come the new catalogs with ever more tempting offerings. Can I find space for a shadbush? An abeliophyllum? Some white pulmonaria? And so on to another white spring. □

Betty Gatewood gardens and edits books in Ossining, New York.

Spring Ephemerals

These flowering perennials announce
the season with a burst of color

by Viki Ferreniea

As winter begins to wane, edging inevitably toward spring, the minds of many gardeners, myself included, are filled with visions of the growing season to come. In particular, we linger on thoughts of the first flowers that will greet us and nudge us into our gardens. I think some of the most engaging of these early plants belong to a group known as the spring ephemerals.

Plants in this group are ephemeral because they have a short growth cycle. The delicate-looking flowers, often white or pastel, and the foliage of these understory, woodland plants emerge in early spring, defying snow in the North and rain in the South. Then the flowers fade and the plants die down and go dormant immediately after their seeds ripen in late spring, making room in the border for other plants, such as ground covers and flowering perennials, to step in and continue the pageant.

The most notable spring ephemerals are familiar bulbs such as tulips, daffodils, crocuses and snowdrops. But other early flowering plants, which may be less well known and less frequently seen in gardens, are equally lovely. Among these lesser-known ephemerals are plants with evocative names such as Virginia bluebells, leopard's bane, anemone, shooting-star, white dog-tooth violet and Dutchman's breeches.

Despite their fragile appearance, spring ephemerals are tough and adaptable plants. The majority of them grow from fleshy, underground structures such as bulbs, corms, tubers or rhizomes. During the plants' brief period of annual growth, their specialized root systems store enough food to provide the energy the plants need to get through the following spring's cycle of flowering and reproduction. Most are hardy as far north as USDA Hardiness Zone 4 (-30°F), but they also tolerate the heat and humidity of the South. And if a cool, shaded place can even be found to plant them in, some can grow in Zone 8.

Growing requirements

Their native environment, coupled with the timing of their growth cycle, provides clues to the cultural requirements of spring ephemerals. The majority of them grow naturally in woodlands. They flower so early in the season that the leaves on the trees and shrubs above them have not yet opened, which means that they are, in fact, growing and flowering in full sun. And it is the warmth of the sun that is vital for them to thrive and complete their growth cycle during the early days of spring. These plants enter dormancy in late spring, when the expanding leaves overhead provide a canopy of protective shade. The shade cools the ground where they are planted and reduces moisture evaporation from the soil during the hot months of summer. As a result, their root systems remain plump and healthy while the plants are dormant.

For spring ephemerals to prosper and spread in a garden setting, they should be grown in the type of soil typically associated with their native woodlands. There the accumulation of leaves creates a friable, humus-rich, dark brown earth. You can meet their needs by planting them in well-drained soil that is rich in organic matter. Cool the soil around them by covering it with a year-round layer of organic mulch, or surround spring ephemerals with plants whose foliage will shade the ground.

Propagation is either by seed or division. To grow spring ephemerals from seed, sow fresh seed (either collected or purchased in the current year) in late spring. Keep the soil shaded and moist throughout the growing season. The best time to move or divide mature spring ephemerals is when the foliage is yellow and withering, a sign that the plants are going dormant.

Because spring ephemerals disappear by the time hot weather arrives, they are suited to growing in a broad range of locations. In all but very hot-summer climates they can be planted in sunny beds or those that receive sun only in the morning. But in hot climates it is advisable to plant them beneath a canopy of taller plants to shade their roots in summer.

I have enjoyed growing spring ephemerals for the past 30 years in gardens in various places where I've lived, including New England, the Southeast and now the Midwest. I will introduce you to six of my favorite ones that will make a showy display in your garden each year.

White dog-tooth violet
(Erythronium albidum)

Elegant, white flowers reminiscent of miniature lilies that sparkle like patches of snow against the last somber tones of winter are reason enough to grow white dog-tooth violet (see top of photo at right). Its flowers stand above 6-in. to 8-in. tall, shining, oval leaves, which are handsomely mottled with silver. To encourage this plant's eagerness to herald spring at the first opportunity, plant its small corms in a warm, protected place, such as a south-facing slope or against a masonry wall.

White dog-tooth violet flourishes in a humusy, moisture-retentive soil in an area that receives summer shade. Under these conditions, this little champion forms small colonies. One of my favorite ways to grow the white dog-tooth violet is among low-growing ground covers such as native gingers (*Asarum* spp.).

European wood anemone
(Anemone nemorosa)

The flowers of this engaging denizen of rich, humusy soils emerge in early spring and are surrounded by 4-in. to 6-in. tall, deeply cut, fern-like foliage. The species has small, cup-shaped, white flowers. There are also a number of lovely selections that bloom in shades of blue and soft pink (see bottom of photo at right).

European wood anemone can form dense colonies that make a wonderful sight when mixed with shade-loving, woodland ground covers such as wild ginger (*Asarum canadense*) and creeping phlox (*Phlox stoloni-fera*), which blooms in shades of white, pink, blue and lavender, and the various primroses.

The snow-white flowers and elegantly mottled leaves of white dog-tooth violet make it a fitting companion for the lavender-blue flowers of this European wood anemone.

Bright yellow, daisy-like flowers and heart-shaped leaves contribute to the charm of leopard's bane, a long-flowering perennial for sunny places.

Cyclamen-like white flowers held high above a rosette of oval leaves give this spring ephemeral its common name of shooting-star.

Leopard's bane (*Doronicum caucasicum*)

Leopard's bane begins a new gardening season with great exuberance. In early spring a 1-ft. to 2-ft. tall basal rosette of apple-green leaves is soon followed by sunny yellow, daisy-like flowers carried on abundant 20-in. to 24-in. tall, flexible stems.

This plant is ideal for a sunny location in the middle of a border, where I like to combine its cheerful, long-lasting splash of yellow with the rich lavender-pink flowers of the hardy geranium 'Claridge Druce' (*Geranium × oxonianum*) and blue bearded iris.

Shooting-star (*Dodecatheon meadia*)

Exquisite flowers with backward-curving petals characterize the eastern native shooting-star. Four to six flowers form a whorl of colors ranging from pale pink or lavender-pink to deep rose and occasionally white on 8-in. to 12-in tall stems in mid- to late spring.

Shooting-star needs moisture-retentive soil. I have always grown it in shady areas or partial shade, but it can also be grown in sun if the soil is amply mixed with humus and never allowed to dry out and bake in the summer.

SOURCES

Seeds and plants of the spring ephemerals mentioned by the author may be found among the following mail-order sources.

Seeds:

New England Wild Flower Society, Garden In The Woods, 180 Hemenway Rd., Framingham, MA 01701, 508-877-7630. Annual dues: $35; members receive list of available seeds and a discount. Seed list only: $2. Minimum order: 5 seed packets.

North American Rock Garden Society, Jaques Mommens, executive secretary, P.O. Box 67, Millwood, NY 10546;. Annual dues: $25; members receive bulletin and list of available seeds. $12.50 for 25 packets of seeds of your choice, 35 packets if you donate any seed.

Plants:

Busse Gardens, 13579 10th St. N.W., Cokato, MN 55321, 612-286-2654.

Carroll Gardens, 444 E. Main Street, P.O. Box 310, Westminster, MD 21158, 410-848-5422. Catalog $3, deductible.

McClure & Zimmerman, 108 W. Winnebago, P.O. Box 368, Friesland, WI 53935, 414-326-4220. Catalog free.

Shady Oaks Nursery, 112 10th Ave. S.E., Waseca, MN 56093, 507-835-5033. Catalog $1.

White Flower Farm, Route 63, Litchfield, CT 06759-0050, 203-496-9600. Individual catalogs free.

Photos: left, Delilah Smittle; right, J. Paul Moore

Dutchman's-breeches is named for its plump, white flowers, which are spaced out along a thin stem. This plant forms a ground cover in early spring if given a moist, shady location.

Dutchman's-breeches
(Dicentra cucullaria)

The delicate, pristine white flowers of Dutchman's-breeches are one of my favorite reminders that spring is here. This native wildflower can be found growing in deciduous woods throughout temperate areas of North America. The plants, which are 4 in. to 6 in. tall, emerge and flower when the air is still brisk and soil is still cold.

Dutchman's-breeches flourishes in richly organic soil, where it multiplies from seed and forms new clumps. It flowers for several weeks in early spring, but once its glossy, black seeds have been dispersed, it slips into dormancy. Because *Dicentra* dies back by summer, it makes a good companion for shade-loving foliage plants, such as astilbes, whose expanding leaves fill in the gaps.

Virginia bluebells is named for its blue, bell-shaped flowers, which nod above a drift of broad, green leaves. Like most early flowering perennials, this spring ephemeral enjoys a moist, woodland environment.

Virginia bluebells (Mertensia virginica)

Everyone who has seen this colorful, native wildflower in early spring is enchanted by its graceful proportions and overall appearance. View it often— its flowers change color constantly. Young buds are deep pink, become suffused with blue as they expand, and finally mature to a deep, sky-blue color in mid-spring. A swathe of fully opened, tubular-shaped blue flowers is set against 12-in. to 15-in. tall plants with broad, gray-green leaves.

When Virginia bluebells are grown as a small group in a shady border or as a drift, the effect is delightful. For optimum growth and flowering, they need a wooded area with rich, moisture-retentive soil that does not dry out completely in summer, especially in warm climates. In fact, they are quite tolerant of wet conditions in the spring, and in the wild I have found them growing in rich, silty soils beside a stream that is subject to early spring flooding. □

Viki Ferreniea is the author of A Gardener's Guide to Growing Wild-flowers in Your Garden *(Random House, Inc.). She grows spring ephemerals in Putnam, Illinois.*

Perennials for Fall

A sampler of flowers that extend the gardening season

by Stephanie Cohen

As summer ends, thoughts of autumn come to mind: that ever-so-subtle nip in the air; the beautiful reds, golds, oranges and purples of fall foliage; the bounty of autumn harvests; traditional football games. For perennial gardeners, autumn also means the end of fighting drought, mean-spirited insects and the neighbor's dog. It's a time to take stock of the past season's triumphs and failures.

But fall is also a time when perennial gardens tend to look messy, overgrown and lackluster. The sight of tired, weather-beaten plants when it's finally cool enough to get out and do something about them often inspires the quick-fix response. We dash off to the garden center and load up on fall-blooming chrysanthemums of every color, size and shape, then plop them randomly into our flower beds. I think there's a better way.

Putting together a fall look

In my garden and in the gardens I design for my clients here in the Philadelphia, Pennsylvania, area, I include perennials that come into their own in autumn. The variety of fall-blooming

Waves of color wash over a perennial border at the New York Botanical Garden designed to shine in autumn. By combining fall-blooming perennials with those that flower earlier, you can have a beautiful border all season.

perennials is astonishing; you could plant an entire garden with nothing but perennials that flower in September, October and November. But since most of us look at our borders all year long, we need to strike a balance between the seasons. Try to give

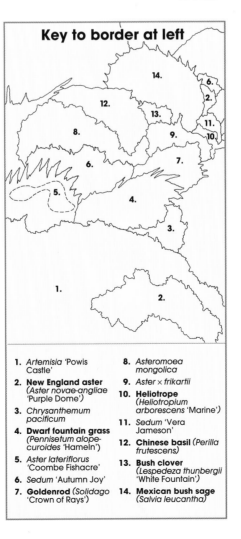

Key to border at left

1. *Artemisia* 'Powis Castle'
2. **New England aster** (*Aster novae-angliae* 'Purple Dome')
3. *Chrysanthemum pacificum*
4. **Dwarf fountain grass** (*Pennisetum alopecuroides* 'Hameln')
5. *Aster lateriflorus* 'Coombe Fishacre'
6. *Sedum* 'Autumn Joy'
7. **Goldenrod** (*Solidago* 'Crown of Rays')
8. *Asteromoea mongolica*
9. *Aster × frikartii*
10. **Heliotrope** (*Heliotropium arborescens* 'Marine')
11. *Sedum* 'Vera Jameson'
12. **Chinese basil** (*Perilla frutescens*)
13. **Bush clover** (*Lespedeza thunbergii* 'White Fountain')
14. **Mexican bush sage** (*Salvia leucantha*)

spring-, summer- and fall-blooming plants each about one-third of the total design. Then you can have a colorful border from spring to hard frost.

For maximum visual impact, plant in drifts. A flowing mass of goldenrods, for example, provides a wash of eye-catching yellow, while a single plant or two can look lost or weedy. Also, try to place three or four perennials that flower at the same time in neighboring drifts to create small garden pictures or vignettes. Scattered drifts can make a garden look spotty.

Fall-flowering perennials aren't the only secret to having an attractive fall border. When I design a garden for season-long interest, I use perennials that I call "eye-foolers," plants that have colorful foliage. They trick the eye into seeing a colorful garden even when little is in bloom. Among my favorite eye-foolers are rue (*Ruta graveolens*), with its cool, ferny, blue-green foliage; *Heuchera* 'Palace Purple', which has red-purple, maple-like leaves; and silver-leaved plants such as artemisias. These plants have beautiful foliage all season long.

Other perennials become eye-foolers only in fall. Both *Bergenia cordifolia* and leadwort (*Ceratostigma plumbaginoides*), for example, have gorgeous, bronze-purple autumn foliage. And the variegated Solomon's seal (*Polygonatum odoratum* 'Variegatum'), a woodland plant, has leaves that turn a marvelous shade of gold with creamy white edges. Keep your eyes open for other perennials with interesting fall foliage. It pays to be imaginative when you're hunting for the last hints of color.

All photos, except where noted: Chris Curless; Illustration: Grace Schaar

A gaggle of pink anemone flowers tumbles over the plant's maple-shaped leaves.

The powder-puff flowers of the white cultivar of hardy ageratum mingle with the last few daisies of a perennial black-eyed Susan. Hardy ageratum grows 2 ft. to 3 ft. tall and survives winter where temperatures do not drop below -20˚F.

Autumn flowers

I have several favorite fall-blooming perennials. Many are tried-and-true, but I also grow some weird but wonderful plants that have earned a place in my garden for the beauty of their late-season display. I'll tell you about six of my fall favorites here. In the next article (pp. 44-47), I'll describe several more. (For mail-order nurseries that carry fall-blooming perennials, see Sources on p. 42.)

Anemones—A fall garden is incomplete without anemones (Anemone spp.). These wonderful, 2-ft. to 3-ft. tall plants seem to explode into bloom in the fall with single, semi-double or double flowers in shades of rose, pink, salmon or white. Held aloft on fragile-looking stems, the flowers and shiny buds add a certain gracefulness at this time of year, while the three-part, maple-shaped leaves are attractive all season long.

Anemones grow best in rich, organic soil in part shade. They are hardy to USDA Hardiness Zone 5 (-20˚F). In hot-summer areas, they need shade during the heat of the afternoon. In my experience, anemones are insect- and disease-free.

There is a wide variety of fall-blooming anemone cultivars. 'Honorine Jo-

bert' is the best white anemone, and 'September Charm', with its silvery pink flowers, is a late-season knockout.

Hardy ageratums—The lovely, fluffy blue flower clusters of hardy ageratum (Eupatorium coelestinum) look like those of its close relative, the low-growing annual ageratum. But the hardy ageratum's flowers open in fall on a plant that grows 2 ft. to 3 ft. tall and is cold-hardy to Zone 5. The hardy ageratum also thrives in milder-winter climates.

Blue is in short supply in fall, a time when warmer hues predominate. Try combining hardy ageratum with yellow goldenrods or rusty pink Sedum 'Autumn Joy'. The hardy ageratum's soft blue flowers make the colors of its neighbors appear to shine all the brighter. If blue is not what you need, hardy ageratum also comes in white (the cultivar name is 'Alba').

I have to sound one note of caution about this wonderful native perennial. Hardy ageratum is just like Brylcreem: "A little dab will do you." Given moist soil in either sun or light shade, hardy ageratum sends out rhizomes (horizontal stems) in all directions. Every year, I give away several pots of stem pieces sliced off the advancing edges, and every year the plant grows to the size it reached the year before. If you fear you won't be able to keep up with hardy ageratum, plant it where it can't maneuver through your garden, or plant it in a large plastic tub with holes cut for drainage and sink the tub into the ground, leaving the rim just above soil level.

Goldenrods—I must put in a plug for an excellent but neglected group of plants, the goldenrods *(Solidago* spp.). I know what you're thinking, but they don't cause hayfever (ragweed, which blooms at the same time, is the real culprit), and they can make great garden plants. It's true that some of the taller goldenrods tend to be aggressive, but there are many shorter goldenrods that have been selected for their good behavior. Try 'Crown of Rays', which has golden yellow flowers on 2 ft. plants, or 'Peter Pan', a slightly taller plant with canary yellow flowers. Almost every garden has room for 'Golden Fleece', a new selection that grows only 2 ft. tall. It looks like a fountain of cascading gold.

Goldenrods are easy to grow, thriving in almost any soil in full sun. Many species and their cultivars survive winters in Zone 3 (-40°F), but they also thrive in climates with milder winters.

If you've never tried a goldenrod, I think you'll be pleasantly surprised. Think how colorful a field of goldenrods can be; then picture what they can do for a fall garden in need of a spark. Goldenrods combine well with other fall-flowering plants, including asters, ornamental grasses and mums. Bring a few flowers into the house; goldenrods make long-lasting cut flowers.

Asters—Fall-blooming asters are today's hot perennials. New cultivars are being introduced almost hourly. It's easy to see why. Asters produce huge numbers of 2-in. wide daisies in colors from pink to purple to white on plants that range in size from low-growing edging plants to towering beauties for the middle or the back of the border.

I like the lower-growing asters best. They don't require pinching or staking the way most of the tall asters do. One of the most beautiful new low-growers is *Aster dumosus* 'Lady in Blue'. It's short, growing only about 16 in. tall, and finely textured, with clear blue flowers. My all-time favorite is *A. novae-angliae* 'Purple Dome'. Its dramatic, deep violet-purple flowers

The goldenrod 'Golden Fleece' weaves gold flowers among the blush pink daisies of *Aster lateriflorus* 'Coombe Fishacre' and the finely cut silver leaves of *Artemisia* 'Powis Castle'. Unjustly maligned for causing hayfever, goldenrods can bring a spark to fall gardens that show the wear and tear of a long, hot summer.

A line of intricate, white-and-purple toad lily flowers runs along the back of an arching stem. Though not the showiest of autumn bloomers, toad lilies reward a closer look.

The bright pink flower spikes of the false dragonhead cultivar 'Vivid' make an attractive contrast in form and color with the white flowers of a late-blooming summer phlox and the yellow blossoms of a coneflower.

gardeners can't miss them. Combine them with ferny shade-lovers, such as astilbes and bleeding-hearts (*Dicentra* spp.), for a nice contrast of foliages.

False dragonheads—For variation in flower form, try false dragonhead (*Physostegia virginiana*). Its small, tubular, pink, purple or white flowers are clustered along branching spikes. On close inspection, you can see that the flowers really do look like the heads of toothy dragons. False dragonhead grows 2 ft. to 4 ft. tall, is hardy to about Zone 4, and tolerates heat and humidity well.

False dragonhead is also commonly called the obedient plant, because if you push the flowers to one side, they stay put. But this vigorous native is anything but obedient. It can spread rapidly through moist garden soil in full sun or part shade. Divide plants every two years or so to keep them from becoming disobedient.

False dragonhead has many cultivars. My favorite is an especially-late-flowering selection called 'Vivid'. I've had its bright pink flowers in my garden as late as November. I also like 'Variegata', a late-blooming cultivar with attractive white-edged foliage and bright, rose-pink flowers.

It's November now; tonight we're expecting the hard freeze that will lay my garden to rest for the winter. But I can't complain. I've enjoyed every minute, from beginning to end. □

Stephanie Cohen designs gardens and teaches horticulture at colleges and botanical gardens in the Philadelphia area. She gardens in Norristown, Pennsylvania.

and compact size—it grows 18 in. tall and wide—make it a choice garden plant (see right corner of photo on facing page). Combine it with goldenrods and dwarf fountain grass (*Pennisetum alopecuroides* 'Hameln') for a beautiful late-fall picture.

Asters thrive in average garden soil in full sun. Many are hardy to Zone 4 (-30°F); most fare best in hot-summer climates if they get some afternoon shade. Divide asters every two or three years to retain their vigor. Slice up a clump, discard the woody center and replant the new, outer growth.

Toad lilies—Toad lilies (*Tricyrtis hirta*) fall into the "interesting, but not showy" category (see photo on p. 41). No one notices them unless you point them out, and even then non-gardeners just shrug their shoulders and say, "so?" But to those of us who love to grow something different, they look exotic. Toad

lilies have arching, 2-ft. to 3-ft. stems. In September, rows of orchid-like white flowers open where the pointed leaves are attached to the stems. If you look closely, you'll see that the blooms are speckled with dark purple.

For something even more unusual, look for *T. formosana*. Its flowers have darker purple spots and a yellow throat, and they last almost three weeks longer than those of *T. hirta*. *T. formosana* grows to less than 2 ft. tall, and it can be invasive in moist soil, spreading by rhizomes just beneath the surface of the soil.

Toad lilies are easy to grow. They thrive in part shade in a moisture-retentive soil. They'll tolerate drier soil, but they won't grow as vigorously. Toad lilies are hardy to Zone 4; with adequate shade, they'll also grow well in hot-summer climates. Plant toad lilies close to a path or in a conspicuous spot so your friends and fellow

SOURCES

The following mail-order nurseries carry most of the fall-blooming perennials described by the author.

Busse Gardens, 13579 10th Street NW, Cokato, MN 55321-9426, 612-286-2654. Catalog $2 (3-yr. subscription), deductible from first order.

Carroll Gardens, 444 East Main Street, P.O. Box 310, Westminster, MD 21158, 410-848-5422. Catalog $2, deductible from first order.

Milaeger's Gardens, 4838 Douglas Avenue, Racine, WI 53402-2498, 800-669-9956. Catalog $1.

Andre Viette Farm & Nursery, Route 1, Box 16, Fisherville, VA 22939, 703-943-2315. Catalog $3.

The purple daisies of *Aster* 'Purple Dome', the rust-colored flower heads of *Sedum* 'Autumn Joy', and the silver leaves of *Artemisia* 'Powis Castle' make a collage of autumn color.

Perennials for a Brilliant Fall Finale

Plants that shine as the garden goes to sleep

Sedums are nearly indestructible. Their tough nature and easy adaptability make them perfect plants for beginners. *Sedum* 'Autumn Joy' creates a colorful portrait with *Aster* 'Alma Potschke' and yarrow. A white phlox and sneezeweed complete the picture.

All photos: Chris Curless

by Stephanie Cohen

Perennial gardeners are glad to see fall arrive. They know they can finish the season with a flourish, not with a whimper, because at this time of year nature puts on its greatest display—reds, golds, yellows and oranges—in a dazzling finale.

In the previous article (pp. 38-43), I told you about some of the workhorses of the fall garden. Here, I'll add other perennials to your list. It's very important to treat fall as an integral part of your overall garden design. Almost one-third of your plants should be picked for their fall flowering or for leaves that have good fall color. Peony leaves bronze, and those of *Bergenia, Ceratostigma* spp. and *Tiarella cordifolia* (foamflower) turn red. Bluestar (*Amsonia hubrectii*) leaves turn a lovely yellow. With proper planning, a perennial garden should be colorful until November.

Fall Favorites

Sedums—Every autumn garden needs sedums. *Sedum* 'Autumn Joy' is a fine garden plant, with its fleshy leaves, bushy form and thick heads of broccolilike flowers that change from green to pink to rust as the season progresses. Some of my other favorites are *Sedum* 'Ruby Glow', with gray-green foliage and pink flowers; *Sedum* 'Vera Jameson', with pink flowers and leaves that are a rich purple; and purple stonecrop (*Sedum maximum* 'Atropurpureum'), which has dark purple leaves and starry white flowers with dark centers. All of these sedums flower from August through fall.

More good choices are variegated showy stonecrop (*Sedum spectabile* 'Variegatum'), which has pink flowers and variegated leaves, and 'Star Dust' showy stonecrop (*Sedum spectabile* 'Star Dust'). October daphne, or October plant (*Sedum sieboldii*), has pink-edged, glaucous blue leaves and pink flowers, and gives the last hint of color in the fall garden. Despite its name, October daphne begins flowering in September.

Besides their more obvious attractions, sedums are "basketball plants"— the kids can tramp on them, Dad can accidentally mow them, but they'll take the abuse and bounce right back. Sometimes when people tell me they've killed sedums, I tell them the only thing left for them is to get plastic flowers. (For more on these plants, see *FG* #35, "Sedums," pp. 55–59.)

Sedums are heat- and drought-tolerant and prefer full sun. An easy perennial for beginners to grow, sedums are low maintenance and need dividing only every three to four years. They're hardy from USDA zones 3 (–40°F) to 9 (20°F).

Monkshoods—Among the excellent monkshoods that offer spires of exceptional beauty is *Aconitum* × *arendsii* with its dark violet, hooded flowers. This perennial is one of the best of the new hybrids—it grows 3 to 4 ft. tall and is self-supporting. It looks great planted with white or pink anemones.

This monkshood likes full sun but will tolerate afternoon shade. It also tolerates moisture but hates wet roots and needs cool nights to really strut its

stuff; it doesn't do well in the South. This cultivar doesn't transplant well, so pick your spot and leave it alone.

Azure monkshood (*Aconitum carmichaelii*), or fall aconitum, displays its dark blue flowers from late summer to early fall. Azure monkshood likes afternoon shade and organic, moisture-retentive soil. Both aconitums are hardy from zones 3 to 7 (0°F.)

The roots, stems and leaves of these plants are poisonous, though they are the source of the drug aconite, used as a heart sedative. In our area, this is one plant the deer do not eat.

Patrinias—Like goldenrods, patrinias are great but underused plants. The jagged pinnate leaves of patrinias are shiny, and the yellow umbels are yarrowlike but more delicate; they look like a mist of yellow. When the flowers fade, their attractive yellow bracts remain showy, and the leaves turn bronzy yellow in autumn.

Patrinia scabiosifolia is available in two types—the Japanese type, which reaches 3 ft. tall, and the Korean type, which can reach 6 ft. tall. *P. villosa* is 3 ft. tall and white-flowered.

A deerproof plant, azure monkshood is an easy beauty to grow in moisture-retentive soil. Also known as fall aconitum, this late-blooming cultivar adds a difficult-to-find fall color.

SOURCES

The following mail-order nurseries carry most of the fall-blooming perennials described by the author.

Busse Gardens, 13579 10th St. NW, Cokato, MN 55321-9426; 612-286-2654. Catalog, $2 (three-year subscription), deductible from first order.

Carroll Gardens, 444 East Main St., P.O. Box 310, Westminster, MD 21158; 410-848-5422. Catalog, $3, deductible from first order.

Milaeger's Gardens, 4838 Douglas Ave., Racine, WI 53402-2498; 800-669-9956. Catalog, $1.

André Viette Farm & Nursery, Route 1, Box 16, Fishersville, VA 22939; 703-943-2315. Catalog, $3.

Patrinias are wonderful with grasses, creating a haze of gold in the fall garden. Planted between *Pennisetum alopecuroides* and *Miscanthus sinensis* 'Gracillimus', patrinias add a colorful accent.

It was still in full bloom in my garden at the beginning of November. It was up to its petioles in fallen leaves, but it was still bravely blooming. Its paniclelike bloom clusters will remind you of the flowers of white snakeroot (*Eupatorium rugosum*).

I love patrinia with grasses—any of the *Miscanthus* species or the beautiful blue mist shrub (*Caryopteris* × *clandonensis*) in the back of the border with boltonia. Patrinia can also be used as a see-through plant, as is *Verbena bonariensis*. In the fall, the foliage of patrinias may turn reddish orange with yellow highlights.

Patrinias flower August through September and make good cut flowers. They are hardy in zones 5 (−20°F) to 8 (10°F). I've read that patrinias grow best in moist, peaty soil in lightly shaded woodlands, but I guess my plant hasn't read the same books I have. It has been in my garden in clay soil and full sun for four years now, and it's thriving.

Boltonia—You can have a real love-hate relationship with boltonia (*Boltonia asteroides*), also known as Bolton's aster. A white daisylike flower with a yellow center, boltonia also has beau-

tiful, slender blue-green foliage. It's big—between 3 and 5 ft. tall—and sometimes the weight of the flowers can make it unwieldy. When you read about these plants, the texts usually say, "may need staking." But this is a gross understatement. A boltonia absolutely needs staking, or you must pinch it severely in early spring, unless you garden in the style of 19th century English horticulturist Gertrude Jekyll and let plants fall where they may. In that case, lean it against something else.

Excellent cultivars include 'Snowbank', which is supposed to reach only 4 ft. tall, although I've never seen it stay quite that short. A pink-blooming cultivar, 'Pink Beauty' doesn't grow quite as vigorously as 'Snowbank' at first. But it does catch up, eventually reaching 5 to 6 ft. tall. Its habit is a bit looser than that of 'Snowbank', but the pale pink flowers of 'Pink Beauty' are a welcome addition to the fall garden.

Boltonias mix well with *Sedum* 'Autumn Joy'; blue salvia (*Salvia azurea* 'Grandiflora'); and anemones such as the semidouble, deep pink 'Margarette' or semidouble, soft pink 'Queen Charlotte'. My favorite combination is boltonia with Russian sage (*Perovskia atriplicifolia*)—the daisies look dramatic against the sage's hazy blue spires.

Besides being so attractive, boltonia is also a tough plant. It holds up well during drought and will grow from zones 4 (−30°F) through 8 (10°F).

Boltonia must be staked; its lush growth can top out at 5 ft. tall. The profusion of white daisylike flowers make it a handsome companion for tall plants such as the cleome, at right.

themum × 'Mei-Kyo') bears very small, dainty, double rose-colored flowers on 18-in.-long stems. I keep it pinched so I get very bushy plants that don't even begin to flower until mid to late October. My other choice is Nippon daisy (*Chrysanthemum nipponicum*). It also flowers from October to first frost and bears large white flowers with yellow-green centers.

These plants need pinching to look their best. If you don't give them a good trim in the spring, they'll get rangy, leggy and woody, eventually reaching 3 to 5 ft. tall. Pinch them hard as early as possible to hold them to a compact 2 to 3 ft. Delaying pinching even until June or July may cause them to bloom too late and be damaged by frost. They need full sun and well-drained soil. I don't fertilize them more than three times a year, or they get too leggy.

Fall can be one of the most colorful, exciting and distinctive seasons in anyone's garden. Remember, with proper planning, a garden can flower from March to November in many areas. Even at the end of the gardening season, the last vivid colors of the garden perennials can be just as pleasing as the first breath of spring.   □

Stephanie Cohen teaches horticulture and plant ecology and gardens in Norristown, Pennsylvania.

It can take partial shade and can tolerate a wide range of soils, although it does best in rich organic soil. Fertilize it early in the spring.

Japanese aster—This handsome plant has a botanical name that changes almost weekly. Now known as *Kalimeris mongolica*, this plant has also been classified as *Asteromoea mongolica*, *Boltonia indica* and *Aster mongolicus*. But whatever you call it, it's a great perennial for fall.

The terrifically floriferous Japanese aster grows to 3 ft. tall but doesn't stand out until suddenly it's covered with white flowers. Its narrow, serrated leaves are not particularly showy, but its pure white petals with bright yellow centers are a perfect foil for other perennials, such as ornamental grasses, rudbeckias and sedums.

Bloom starts in midsummer and doesn't let up until a hard frost. Last year, mine flowered into November. I have never seen mildew on this plant; it withstands drought and humidity and is hardy from zones 5 to 9. Japanese aster needs full sun, but gardeners in the South may want to give it morning sun and dappled shade in the afternoon. A low-maintenance perennial, Japanese aster thrives in a loamy garden with minimal fertilizing.

Chrysanthemums—If pressed very hard, I'll confess that I actually like two chrysanthemums. 'Mei-Kyo' (*Chrysan-*

Japanese aster makes a graceful foil for *Sedum* 'Autumn Joy'. Japanese aster boasts a long season of bloom and tolerates drought and humidity.

My favorite mum, Nippon daisy, or Montauk daisy, doesn't bloom until October. A hard pinching in the spring creates a full, bushy plant.

Plants for Winter Gardens
Nine choices to enliven cold-weather doldrums

by Viki Ferreniea

I used to live in the Northeast, where it was hard work to have anything interesting in the garden during the seemingly-endless, bleak winter months. By contrast, only one year after starting my garden here in South Carolina, I was delighted to count 115 kinds of plants either in flower or with foliage in good condition in early December. It's exhilarating to sample the diversity of plants that can be grown here and to see how they perform in this climate. Now I look forward to winter as I once did to summer.

My garden is a blend of plants—bulbs, hardy herbaceous perennials, grasses, shrubs and vines, along with some carefully chosen annuals and tender perennials. And much as I enjoy flowers, especially fragrant ones, I always look for additional reasons to grow a plant, such as attractive foliage, unusual bark or branch patterns, or colorful fruit or berries. These draw me out to savor and explore the garden even in December and January. I'll introduce nine of my favorite plants for winter interest in this article. Some are familiar, some are unusual, but all are worth seeking out and growing. Ask for them at your local garden center, or mail-order them from specialty nurseries.

These plants do well for me in USDA Zone 8 (winter lows of 10° to 20°F), but they can tolerate varying degrees of cold. Remember that hardiness is affected by available moisture, wind, snow cover or lack of it, elevation, the duration of very cold periods, and so on. A zone designation is just a guideline, taken too literally by beginning gardeners and treated with great skepticism by "old hands." Many plants survive outside their zone if placed in just the right site.

Christmas rose (*Helleborus niger*)

Zone 3. Christmas rose lives up to its name in England, where it flowers around the holiday season. In this country, it can bloom anytime from early December to March, depending on where it's grown. The clear-white flowers do indeed resemble delicate single roses, sparkling dramatically against the dark-green leaves. These flowers last for a long time and seem indifferent to the cold, rain or snow that often descends upon them.

One plant grows to form a knee-high clump. Volunteer seedlings often augment the mother plant, and in time the handsome, almost leathery foliage can become a distinctive ground cover. Christmas rose needs deep, rich organic soils that don't dry out in summer, and a shady location. Typically, the further north it's grown, the more light it will tolerate.

Japanese Solomon's-seal and astilbes are good companions for Christmas rose. So are the Japanese primroses—the pastel-colored ones make an especially nice display against the dark Christmas-rose foliage.

Beautyberry (*Callicarpa bodinieri*)

Zone 6. Beautyberry's finest display comes in fall and winter, when shiny magenta berries develop in bunches like miniature grapes. In spring, clusters of white and purple flowers fill the axils of the dark-green leaves. This is an undemanding shrub that will grow in sun or in light shade, and which is happy in ordinary garden soils. It grows to approximately 8 ft. to 10 ft. in height.

Mature plants make good specimens alone, or they can be combined with the white-berried *Callicarpa americana* 'Alba' for added sparkle. The dark foliage of beautyberry makes a good background for a mixed border of grasses and variegated plants.

Variegated Japanese sedge (*Carex morrowii* 'Aureovariegata')

Zone 5. This plant forms clumps of swirling 12-in. leaves that are pale, creamy yellow edged in green. It makes a wonderful edging for a path or bed, and it will brighten a dark corner in summer or winter. This plant is easy to grow in sun or shade, and requires only good garden soil and an annual shearing. Cut back the old foliage each spring to encourage vigorous new growth.

This photo shows variegated Japanese sedge against a background of epimediums. The plant also looks striking in combination with black-leaved lilyturf, or underplanted with white crocuses.

Witch hazels (*Hamamelis* spp.)

Zone 4. A shady site is best for all the witch hazels and essential in the South. But in January through March (depending on where you live), these plants bloom happily in full sun. Most witch hazels have delicate flowers that are produced in abundance and make a welcome display at a time of year when the garden can be bleak. This photo shows witch hazel 'Sunburst', a showstopper with masses of streamerlike petals. The 2-in.-wide flowers are sweetly fragrant, too, and they're good to cut and force indoors.

Witch hazels grow as large shrubs or small trees. They need rich, humusy, moisture-retentive soil and deep watering during droughts, but are generally undemanding. The leaves are attractive all summer, and many witch hazels have lovely fall color.

Heavenly bamboo (*Nandina domestica*)

Zone 6. Although its growth habit is reminiscent of bamboo, this is actually a shrub with woody stems. Its rich, dark evergreen foliage makes a glossy backdrop for the plumes of white flowers that appear in spring and the brilliant scarlet berries of fall and winter. Heavenly bamboo grows 10 ft. to 12 ft. tall and makes a stately specimen, a carefree hedge, or a companion plant in a perennial border. Because of its upright growth habit, it's well suited for tight spaces or near walkways. Dwarf forms are ideal for growing in containers or in small patio gardens.

Heavenly bamboo does well in sun or shade. In areas with very hot, dry summers, supply mulch and occasional watering to keep it vigorous and healthy.

Kuma bamboo (*Sasa veitchii*)

Zone 6. The striking creamy-white leaf edges of this beautiful dwarf bamboo add a wonderful splash of color to a winter garden. Kuma bamboo is evergreen in the South—this picture was taken the last week in January. The new leaves start out green in summer, and their edges turn white in fall with the onset of cool weather.

Kuma bamboo grows 3 ft. to 5 ft. tall. It forms a fine airy ground cover and does better than most plants in dry shade. It spreads rapidly in rich soil, so choose a location where you can enjoy its beauty without encountering maintenance problems.

This dwarf bamboo looks good in front of taller bamboos, as shown here, or under the shade of upright-growing trees such as stewartia and coral bark maple. Consider meadow rues and lilies as other companions for this unique plant.

Winter daphne (*Daphne odora* 'Aureomarginata')

Zone 7. This evergreen winter-flowering shrub brings pure delight to the southern garden. The glossy foliage, which is rich green broadly edged with creamy yellow, makes a colorful display all year. But the true glory comes from the flowers that are deep pink in bud, opening to white flushed with pink, and maturing to rich velvety white. On warm days, their delicious fragrance fills the garden.

This species of daphne must have shade and a rich soil. It resents any kind of root disturbance, so once planted it's best left alone and mulched well. It is compact and grows slowly to a mature height of 4 ft. to 5 ft. It's a perfect companion for the winter-flowering cyclamens, or for the winter-flowering cherry (*Prunus subhirtella* 'Autumnalis'), which blooms from late fall to April here.

Autumn fern (*Dryopteris erythrosora*)
Zone 5. Beautiful throughout the year with
glossy 24-in.-high fronds, this fern's most
spectacular display comes in early spring
when the coppery-colored new growth
appears. Autumn fern is one of the easiest
ferns to grow, but needs a humusy,
moisture-retentive soil and shouldn't be
allowed to dry out.

A single specimen looks good as a
complement to spring bulbs, especially
the bright yellows and whites of
narcissus. Planted in groups, autumn
fern makes a striking ground cover. Try
it with cream- or white-variegated
hostas, or as an underplanting beneath
high-branching shrubs such as witch
hazel, enkianthus or winterberry.

Carolina jessamine (*Gelsemium
rankinii*)
Zone 7. With the exception of clematis,
vines are sadly overlooked in American
gardens. The Carolina jessamine is a
lovely winter-flowering vine. Its dark
evergreen leaves and stems have a
distinctive plum-colored hue, a striking
contrast to its butter-yellow flowers. Unlike
its more familiar cousin *G. sempervirens*,
G. rankinii reblooms in the fall.

Carolina jessamine grows as well in
not-too-heavy shade as in sun, and
makes a good covering for fences, walls
or arbors. It's a trouble-free vine that can
climb 10 ft. to 20 ft., or be kept compact
by pruning. I interplant mine with white-
and pastel-flowering clematis, which are
enhanced by the jessamine's foliage
color. In the summer, Carolina jessamine
makes a good backdrop for sun- or
shade-loving perennials. ☐

*Viki Ferreniea is assistant horticultural
director for Wayside Gardens in South
Carolina.*

Long-Lived Perennials

Undemanding plants that thrive for decades

The fall explosion of reds and yellows does not signal the end for Lancaster geranium; it is hardy down to −30°F.

by Dorothy J. Pellett

Sustainable is such a popular word that it could be suspected of being the buzzword of the '90s. In the sphere of agriculture that pertains to food crops, sustainable signifies methods of raising a crop without negative impact on the soil or water. It means using plants that don't need frequent applications of pesticides, fertilizers or water after their roots are established. How can this idea be applied to perennials?

Many gardeners choose plants for their flower color, texture, use as a cut flower or newly bred characteristics. After several years of experimenting with plants for my Vermont nursery (which specializes in less common perennials), I have discovered that some bloomed profusely but were short-lived, while others added the perfect color but required frequent division.

I have found some plants that stand out, ones that I would always want to include in a garden if I ever had to relocate. For me, these are the plants that live for decades when located in a proper site, plus display one or more other superior traits of flower or foliage. They require little use of pesticides.

Lancaster geranium—hardy and drought tolerant

Success is a natural outcome when planting and growing Lancaster geranium (*Geranium sanguineum* var. *striatum*). I was introduced to it at the age of 12 when I visited a garden center and asked for a perennial that was good for a rock garden. The happy choice encouraged an interest both in gardening and in hardy geraniums. At least 20 different species and cultivars of hardy geranium (not the annually planted *Pelargonium*) will thrive in my Vermont garden.

Lancaster geranium, hardy to USDA Hardiness Zone 3 (–40°F) remains attractive without flopping, surviving periods of drought and displaying a sheet of 1-inch-wide pink flowers in June (photo, right). Each light pink petal

Siberian irises thrive with a good source of moisture. Protect them from drought their first year.

Lancaster geranium survives drought and harsh winters. It flowers in June in New England.

is enhanced by reddish purple veins, to which the term "striatum" refers. Many of the leaves turn bright red-orange in fall and keep their color for weeks (photo, facing page). A system of underground rhizomes contributes to its perseverance in dry weather.

The planting site should be sunny for more than half a day. Although its natural habitat is on hillsides underlain with limestone, it grows vigorously here in soils of pH 5.8 to 6.5. Its cut-leafed foliage is neat all summer, with occasional later blooms. Lancaster geranium mixes well with low-growing plants with pointed leaves.

Siberian iris—carefree when given proper start

Siberian irises (*Iris sibirica*) are familiar in mass plantings; as individual clumps for the dramatic effect of their upright foliage; in formal rows; or as informal additions to waterside gardens. Most contemporary cultivars of Siberian iris, as well as the species itself, are durable in the garden. Roots of established clumps grow so deeply that they are recommended for helping to control erosion on sloping areas. It is hardy from zones 3 to 9 (20°F).

Iris breeders have brought us blooms of lavender, light blue, lavender-pink, yellow-and-white bicolor (top photo, left), and dappled blends. The flowers have upright petals, or standards, and three other petals called "falls". Most are 2 to 3 feet tall. Two free-blooming shorter ones are 'Little White' at 15 inches and the light blue 'Baby Sister', only 10 to 12 inches tall.

Despite their native habitat, near a source of water, these irises do not demand moist spaces; they thrive in the average perennial garden, calling for at least a half day of sun. But they are not a practical choice for shallow soil that dries out quickly. The most important element in establishing Siberian irises is to protect them from drought for one season after planting. When their roots have grown deep and sturdy, the plants will have enough stamina to tolerate most conditions.

It is not necessary to divide Siberian irises for many years, but if you want more plants, divide irises in early spring or late summer. Protect the divisions from drying out before replanting.

Photos: top, Lynne Harrison; bottom, F. Robert Wesley

The pasque flower is undamaged by morning frost, which is often present when it blooms in April.

Pasque flower—Deep roots are the secret of its longevity

Fragile-appearing but tough, European pasque flower (*Pulsatilla vulgaris*) has feathery leaves that hold the dew and sparkle as though frosted with ice crystals (photos, above and right). In my garden, there often are ice crystals in the morning when this plant (hardy from Zone 4b [–25°F] to Zone 8 [10°F]) blooms in late April and early May, but neither ice nor late snow is harmful.

The furry, unopened buds nestle in a circle of leaves near the ground. The stem elongates between flowers and leaves, and below the upper leaf circle. The blooms are often a foot above the ground by the time the fluffy seed heads take their place.

The only time I experienced failure with *Pulsatilla vulgaris* was when I planted one in a poorly drained spot, reminding me that the most important factor for sustainability is choosing a proper site. Pasque flower thrives in sun or light shade in well-drained soils, where its long, fleshy roots go deep enough to use water not available to more shallow-rooted plants—a characteristic shared by most long-lived perennials.

The pasque flower blooms in shades of dark red and purple, or lavender and white (photo, above). I allow the attractive seed heads to remain; the

Not as fragile as it looks, the pasque flower is extremely long-lived if given adequate drainage.

SOURCES

The following mail-order nurseries offer most of the long-lived perennials mentioned in this article:

André Viette Farm and Nursery, Rte. 1 Box 15, Fishersville, VA 22939; 703-943-2315. Catalog, $3.

Busse Gardens, 5873 Oliver Ave. SW, Cokato, MN 55321-3601; 800-544-3192. Catalog, $2 (deductible from order).

Carroll Gardens, P.O. Box 310, Westminster, MD 21158; 800-638-6334. Catalog, $3.

Fieldstone Gardens, Inc., 620 Quaker Ln., Vassalboro, ME 04989-9713; 207-923-3836. Catalog, $2.

resulting seedlings can be transplanted and may surprise you with new variations in color.

'Alexander's White' candytuft— a profuse spring bloomer

In my garden, 'Alexander's White' (*Iberis sempervirens*) stands out from most other perennial candytuft cultivars in terms of floriferousness, density of bloom, clarity of the white flowers and ability to thrive in a location for many years.

At bloom time, during the first half of May, this cultivar appears to be a solid sheet of bright white (top photo, facing page). The plant, hardy in zones 4 to 8 (–30°F to 10°F), is a subshrub, with its older stems becoming sinewy or almost woody at their base. Side branches add to its fullness. Flower stalks that are upright and nearly the same height create an effect that is neat but not formal.

I purchased my original plant 15 years ago. Because I have taken cuttings from it each year after blooming, I have had numerous new plants to test in various locations. The plant size can be controlled by trimming off half the length of each new shoot and removing the outer branches lying on the ground. Removing old flower heads will also bring back its tidy form. At least a half day of sun and good drainage are its basic needs.

After every winter but one, my original plant of 'Alexander's White' appeared with green leaves as the snow melted. One year, however, when the leaves did not appear, I thought that an unusually cold winter had brought about its demise. But after two weeks, new shoot growth signaled that it had survived. Where snow cover is uncertain, a covering of lightweight fir or pine branches laid over candytuft plants in autumn will help to prevent browning of leaves.

Boltonia—last perennial to bloom in the Northeast

As I observed the effects of an early April snowfall one year, the fluff of snow hiding an arborvitae outside the window reminded me of the white cover of blooms on *Boltonia asteroides* 'Snowbank' in October. Its appearance is similar to that of an abundantly blooming white aster, but its leaves are unblemished by the rust or mildew that may bother asters.

Don't expect to find it within specified boundaries 10 or even 3 years later. Not really a rampant grower, it simply sends out spring offshoots with so much vigor that it flourishes in adjoining spaces as well. Give it room to colonize in a naturalized setting in full sun, perhaps at the western edge of a deciduous woodland, and it will need little attention except to remove competing grasses. It is also useful within the perennial garden or border for its harmonious gray-green foliage and surprising number of 1-inch-wide white daisies (photo, right). It can be kept in bounds by division or by removing some of the outer shoots.

Hardy from zones 4 to 9, 'Snowbank' grows 4 feet tall. This cultivar was named at the New England Wild Flower Society's Garden in the Woods in 1938. Current director David Longland suggests cutting it back in July (in Massachusetts) if you wish to have bloom on compact 18-inch-high plants. When the shoots are about 15 inches tall, remove the tips of the shoots.

Even without trimming, the stout stems support the mass of frost-tolerant flowers with no staking. Bloom time varies from late August in southern gardens to October in the Northeast, where it is the last perennial in full bloom.

Hosta 'Krossa Regal'—success under adverse conditions

Amid the striking contrasts and intricate color combinations of variegated hostas today, the ability of the monochromatic 'Krossa Regal' to grow in adverse conditions makes it a top choice as a sustainable perennial. Its large, upright, gray-green leaves bestow a certain elegance when used as a background or focal point in the border (bottom photo, right).

Although I believe hostas belong in partial shade, I have seen this one look remarkably good after a summer in nearly full sun in northern states. Its tough leaves resist slugs and spring frosts; two more reasons to consider it worry-free. It will look its best if occasionally given a thorough watering during a drought.

'Alexander's White' candytuft has bloomed 15 years straight for the author, displaying a remarkable ability to adapt to its location.

Boltonia asteroides 'Snowbank' needs room to colonize. Blooming in October, it is the last perennial in flower in the author's garden.

Hosta 'Krossa Regal' thrives in both full sun and shade. Its tough leaves resist slugs and spring frosts.

There is a white-edged sport of 'Krossa Regal' that has been named 'Regal Splendor'. During the five years that I have grown this sport, it has shown promise of having all of the adaptability of its parent.

Arabis sturii—25 years old and still going strong

The same rock cress (Arabis sturii) plants have resided in my sunny rock garden for more than 25 years, unfazed by cold or snow-filled winters. If the soil is well-drained, this Arabis (USDA Hardiness Zone 4 [–30°F]) grows equally well on steep or level ground and spreads slowly into a dark green carpet studded with clusters of white flowers 4 to 6 inches high in the spring.

Short underground stolons are the means of its spread, but it is never invasive. Rock cress is effective for softening edges in front of a border. It should be kept separated from the lawn area, however, or grass will make its way in and be difficult to remove.

In my garden, it is more dependably hardy and more compact in form than most creeping phlox. If winter winds cause some leaves to brown, new leaves will appear early in spring. Arabis procurrens is a very similar, although slightly larger, species.

Good beginnings lead to permanent vigor

Using plants of sustainable character need not restrict us to the less well-known perennials. Whatever plants we select, helping them to become well established will allow them to last for a long time. One key to successful long-term culture of Siberian irises and hostas is making the initial effort to deep-dig the soil and add manure or organic matter before planting.

Even as I am heartened by growing perennials that stay with me season after season, I find that the challenge of cultivating more difficult ones is part of the appeal of gardening. Whether hard-to-grow or easily contented, most perennials can benefit from application of ideas from those we call sustainable. □

Dorothy J. Pellett gardens and owns a wholesale nursery in Charlotte, VT.

Graceful Grasses
for Small Spaces

These striking accent plants bring ballet to static gardens

Background dancers: The windward swaying of Karl Foerster's feather reed grass sets this garden combination of grass and black-eyed Susans into motion. This reed grass is one of several versatile, noninvasive grasses with foliage that remains under 4 ft. tall.

Photo: Susan Kahn

by Harriet L. Cramer

I'm captivated by the sight and sound of ornamental grasses swaying sensually in the breeze. Their textures, shapes, sizes, and subtle foliage and flower colors often remain interesting and attractive through the early months of winter. Though often thought to be huge, sprawling and invasive, a great many ornamental grasses, in fact, work very well in small gardens or otherwise confined spaces.

Ornamental grasses are tough plants, generally resistant to damage from insects, animals and disease. Even deer seem to find them unappetizing. In my garden and in the gardens I've designed for others, I have experimented with different grasses. I have been impressed with the performance of five in particular. These grasses do not require fertilization or other special care, and most tolerate a wide range of soil and weather conditions. (For information on ordering these grasses by mail, see Sources on p. 60.) All remain attractive over a remarkably long period of time regardless of heat, drought or less-than-ideal soil. Their subtly colored summer foliage gives way to buff-colored autumn foliage and seed heads that linger after frost. (For more information, see "Comparisons of five small grasses" on p. 58.)

'Karl Foerster'
(Calamagrostis × acutiflora)

If I were compelled to use only one ornamental grass in my garden, I would not hesitate to choose Karl Foerster's feather reed grass. This is an exceptionally versatile plant that remains attractive longer than any other grass. It grows from USDA Hardiness Zone 5 (−20°F) to Zone 9 (20°F), and may even remain evergreen in areas with mild winters. 'Karl Foerster' is a cool-season grass with lush green foliage that, like that of other cool-season grasses, begins to grow in early spring, usually in March here in Pennsylvania.

Unlike most cool-season grasses, 'Karl Foerster' never burns out (bleaches) in the summer heat. In June, the arching green foliage reaches its ultimate height of about 2 ft. 'Karl Foerster' then produces 4- to 5-ft.-tall reddish mauve flower heads, called "panicles," on long, straight stems, which dance gracefully with the wind. By mid August the feathery panicles have elongated into narrow, strawlike seed heads. The seed heads remain ornamental through late winter.

Feather reed grasses such as 'Karl Foerster' prefer well-drained soil and full sun, though they will tolerate a bit of shade. They can withstand heat and drought and are, by and large, pest- and disease-resistant; foliage rust may occur if the plants are spaced very close together. Propagate 'Karl Foerster' only by division because its seeds are not viable.

A glowing backdrop: Golden flower heads shimmer above the fine, silvery green foliage of 'Yaku Jima'. This small grass can fit into even modest borders.

Long after other herbaceous perennials have finished flowering and have been ruined by frost, 'Karl Foerster' remains attractive and upright, the flower heads providing a much needed vertical accent. The sensually swaying flower heads have a distinctly primordial sensibility in both sight and sound. The low, deep green foliage and buff-colored inflorescences combine perfectly with almost any imaginable plant. I am fond of using this *Calamagrostis* with the cultivated Joe-Pye weed (*Eupatorium maculatum* 'Gateway'), *Salvia guaranitica* 'Argentine Skies' or black-eyed Susan (*Rudbeckia hirta*). 'Karl Foerster' also makes a wonderful hedge or screen, which I find more interesting than the ubiquitous privet. The erect habit and long season of interest of 'Karl Foerster' make it an ideal container plant, and its inflorescences are excellent for flower arrangements.

'Yaku Jima'
(*Miscanthus sinensis*)

While lovely in form and flower, many *Miscanthus sinensis* cultivars are simply too large for residential gardens. *Miscanthus sinensis* 'Yaku Jima' was one of the first relatively small cultivars to be introduced. I like 'Yaku Jima' a great deal because it stays attractive for a long time. It is reliably hardy through Zone 6 (–10°F), tolerates light shade, and combines easily with herbaceous and woody plants.

'Yaku Jima' is notable for its fine, silvery green foliage. It is a clump-forming, warm-season grass with the typically upright habit of the species. Like other warm-season grasses, 'Yaku Jima' begins growing in early May, and by early summer the foliage reaches its ultimate height of 3 to 4 ft. In August its delicate reddish flower heads begin to bloom, rising from slightly above to 1 ft. above the foliage. By early fall, the whisklike seed heads become golden. After frost, the entire plant takes on a golden cast.

Like other miscanthus, 'Yaku Jima' prefers full sun but is undemanding with regard to soil type. It thrives in hot, dry weather. Propagate 'Yaku Jima' by division in the spring.

There are various landscape uses for 'Yaku Jima'. A single specimen in a container is highly pleasing from late spring through the following winter. The small stature of this grass also makes it suitable for a modest perennial border. I like to combine its delicate foliage with brightly colored and coarse-leaved plants such as rosy-leaf sage (*Salvia involucrata*), *Verbena bonariensis,* New England aster (*Aster novae-angliae* 'Alma Potschke') or *Salvia coccinea* 'Lady in Red'. When planted by a pool, 'Yaku Jima' has a softening effect. It is also ideal as a low hedge or ground cover.

Formosan miscanthus
(*Miscanthus transmorrisonensis*)

I am mystified as to why Formosan miscanthus is not a better known grass. This species is remarkably floriferous, and the sight of its tall, elegant panicles waving in the wind will convince even the most rabid skeptic of the value of ornamental grasses.

Formosan miscanthus has a pleasingly upright shape. Even at 3 to 4 ft. tall, its foliage never needs staking. The foliage is long, narrow and a shimmering shade of silver-green. It sometimes stays evergreen well into January. The flowers shoot up in early August, rising 3 ft. to nearly 3½ ft. above the lustrous foliage. The open, whisklike flowers turn from a pinkish tan color to a silvery white, and to buff tan, as other grasses do, by fall.

The hardiness of Formosan miscanthus is not thoroughly established, but it is thought to be hardy only to Zone 6B (–5°F). This ornamental grass thrives in full sun or light shade, and prefers moist soil. In extremely dry conditions, the leaf tips may turn brown. Formosan miscanthus is a clump-forming grass that is easy to start from seed, and it can also be propagated by division in spring.

A practical reason to use this warm-season grass is to mask the dying foliage of spring-flowering bulbs. A garden that I helped to design at the University of Pennsylvania's Morris Arboretum combines Formosan miscanthus with the blue-flowered *Buddleia* 'Lochinch'. This combination is not only colorful but also appealing because monarch and other butterflies, which are enamored of 'Lochinch', also like to perch on the ornamental grass. Formosan miscanthus and 'Lochinch' work well in small gardens because the flowering grass and

Comparisons of five small grasses

Foliage of these noninvasive grasses ranges in height from 8 in. to 4 ft. tall. **Flower heads** rise from just above the foliage to 3½ ft. higher than the plant, depending on the species.

'Karl Foerster' 'Yaku Jima' 'Heavy Metal' Formosan miscanthus

'Elijah Blue'

6 ft.
5 ft.
4 ft.
3 ft.
2 ft.
1 ft.
0 ft.

Illustration: Rosalind L. Wanke

Whisklike flowers form a delicate foil: Silver-green Formosan miscanthus enhances the flowers of Joe-Pye weed, cleome and bloodflower.

woody shrub are both quite compact. Formosan miscanthus' small size also makes it an excellent grass to plant with dwarf conifers, in a perennial border, as a hedge or in a container.

'Heavy Metal'
(Panicum virgatum)

Those familiar with our native switch grass will be startled by the sight of this upright, bluish gray cultivar. 'Heavy Metal' is a warm-season grass that grows from Zone 5 to Zone 9. It starts to grow in mid to late May, really takes off once the weather warms up, and by late June attains its full height of 3 to 4 ft. From July onward, cloudlike heads of tiny, pinkish tan flowers are held about 1 ft. above the

powder blue foliage, giving the impression of an ethereal haze. The foliage remains erect even after heavy rain. By late fall, 'Heavy Metal' turns bright yellow. It becomes buff, or straw-colored, after the first frost and remains so through winter.

A tough plant, 'Heavy Metal' thrives in almost any soil as long as it grows in full sun. It is neither invasive nor self-sowing. Plants grown from seed may revert to the green foliage of the species, so propagate by division. Cut it back to just a few inches tall once winter foliage is no longer attractive.

Erect and floriferous habit, and colorful foliage, make 'Heavy Metal' an ideal landscape plant. The 2-ft.-wide clumps of this grass fit into most perennial borders. Its powder blue foliage

is an excellent foil for brightly colored flowers, such as thin-leaf sunflower (Helianthus decapetalus) and Mexican sunflower (Tithonia rotundifolia) or Cleome hassleriana 'Rose Queen'.

'Heavy Metal' combines to great effect with fruiting shrubs, such as winterberry (Ilex verticillata) or heavenly bamboo (Nandina domestica). And even a single specimen in a container or placed against a wall can look remarkable. Its airy, pinkish red panicles look wonderful and seem to last forever in fresh or dried arrangements.

'Elijah Blue'
(Festuca cinerea)

I was never particularly impressed by ornamental blue fescues. The blue

SOURCES

Among them, the following sources offer the ornamental grasses described in this article.

Kurt Bluemel, Inc., 2740 Green Lane, Baldwin, MD 21013-9525; 410-557-7229. Catalog, $3; minimum order, $25.

Carroll Gardens, 444 E. Main St., P.O. Box 310, Westminister, MD 21158, 410-848-5422. Catalog, $3, refundable.

Limerock Ornamental Grasses, Inc., RD1, Box 111-C, Port Matilda, PA 16870; 814-692-2272. Catalog, $3; $5 shipping charge for orders under $20.

A cooling influence: The tiny flowers and blue-green foliage of 'Heavy Metal' cool the warmer tones of the yellow-green pines in the foreground.

of summer as it does in early spring when the new foliage emerges.

This adaptable fescue grows from Zone 4 (–30°F) to Zone 9; its neat, tufted clumps of foliage reach 8 in. to 10 in. in height. In July, it forms stiff, upright, 18- to 24-in.-tall straw-colored panicles. Like all fescues, it requires full sun and well-drained, not overly rich soil. Propagate by division because seed-grown plants may not retain the blue color. Cut back the old foliage before growth begins in spring.

'Elijah Blue' is outstanding planted as a low-growing accent plant in a rock garden, in a perennial border, as a path edging or in a container. It is especially effective alongside plants with markedly different textures and colors. Its cool blue foliage looks fantastic against red-tipped Japanese blood grass (*Imperata cylindrica*) or next to the delicate green foliage of *Coreopsis verticillata* 'Moonbeam'.

Maintenance is minimal

Spring is the time to do the minimal routine maintenance ornamental grasses require. Cut them back before new growth begins. It's also the time to plant them because fall-planted grasses can heave out of the ground when it freezes. Every few years, in mid to late spring, lift and divide clumps that look open and dead in the center.

The design possibilities for these intriguing plants are limitless. Try them, especially in smaller spaces, where their presence can be dramatic. ∎

Harriet Cramer is a garden designer, and she writes and lectures about horticultural subjects in Philadelphia.

foliage was attractive in early spring but by July tended to brown out miserably from heat and humidity. Plantings of ornamental fescues as a ground cover struck me as especially unsatisfying because they are clump-forming and never knit together. Mass plantings of these fescues seemed flat, stiff and unnatural.

I was sold on ornamental fescues when I discovered *Festuca cinerea* 'Elijah Blue'. This cultivar has outstanding, powder blue, needle-thin foliage that looks as good in the heat

For the front of the border: Short tufts of blue, needle-thin foliage topped with feathery flowers make 'Elijah Blue' a fine edging plant.

Photo: Susan Kahn

The yellow stars and scalloped leaves of green-and-gold carpet the floor of a woodland garden. Along with other native ground covers, green-and-gold offers a distinctive and attractive alternative to traditional favorites such as pachysandra and ivy.

Ground Covers for Shade

Native plants brighten dark, dry corners

by Martha Oliver

If your garden has a shady nook where you'd like to spread a carpet of green, you have more choices than you may think. Garden centers tend to offer the big three shade-tolerant

ground covers: vinca, pachysandra and English ivy. All are imports that have proved their mettle here and abroad over many years, but I'd like to recommend some alternatives—North American natives that have beautiful spring flowers as well as attractive foliage.

These ground covers deserve a place in your garden. In their native range, they are long-lived and well

adapted to our variable weather conditions. Native ground covers are not necessarily superior to exotics, but chances are good they'll acclimate to your garden's growing conditions. Under deciduous trees, in the informal woodland garden, on the north or east side of a house, or as a carpet under spring bulbs, native ground covers offer hardiness, distinctive leaf shapes and freedom from pests. But the primary reason to grow them is simply because they're beautiful.

Which are the best native ground covers for shade? As amateur gardeners and owners of a small perennials nursery in western Pennsylvania, my husband and I have grown a number of natives over the past 20 years that make excellent ground covers for problem spots. The following are some of our favorites. Although these plants are all native to the eastern half of North America, gardeners in many other areas should be able to grow them by paying attention to their basic needs.

Golden stars all summer long

As beautiful and adaptable as green-and-gold (*Chrysogonum virginianum*) is, I can't imagine why it's not more common in the garden. Its deep green, oval leaves are complemented by myriads of five-rayed yellow daisies that look like tiny stars. Most shade-loving ground covers flower only in spring, but in cool, moist shade, green-and-gold can flower on and off all summer, starting in May. [For more on green-and-gold and other long-blooming perennials, see pp. 70-75.]

In loose garden soil, green-and-gold spreads quickly by underground runners and prostrate stems that root where they touch the soil, soon forming a starry mat about 8 in. to 10 in. tall. Green-and-gold also spreads by seeds, but not enough in my experience to give me any misgivings. Hardy to Zone 5 (-20°F) in the North, green-and-gold will also thrive in shady sites in the Deep South.

Green-and-gold appears to be a variable plant. Some catalogs offer spreading forms (often under the name *C. virginianum australe*); others offer forms that stay put. There are also green-and-golds of varying height. Read catalog descriptions or plant labels carefully to be sure you're getting what you want.

A carpet of phlox

Gardeners who love tall border phlox are sure to appreciate its diminutive, shade-tolerant relative, creeping phlox (*Phlox stolonifera*). Creeping phlox has small, oval leaves and grows barely 3 in. tall. It advances by sending runners out in every direction, like spokes on a wheel. Everywhere a runner takes root, it sends up a 10-in. to 12-in. tall stem that bears five-lobed flowers in May. Creeping phlox flowers come in a variety of colors, from deep

The bright white flowers of the creeping phlox cultivar 'Bruce's White' almost hide the plant's foliage for two weeks in spring. Creeping phlox spreads by runners to form a mat just 3 in. tall under deciduous trees or in the shade of a house.

blue to white to pink, with a range of lavenders and deep purples in between. Among my favorites are the orange-blossom-scented 'Bruce's White', from the Great Smoky Mountains, and 'Fran's Purple', a violet-flowered selection that popped up as a seedling in a Connecticut garden.

The many colors of creeping phlox allow for lovely garden combinations. Try mixing its purple cultivars with the bright, four-petaled, yellow flowers of the native wood poppy (*Stylophorum diphyllum*), or its pale lavender forms with either soft yellow primroses or the soft pink-flowered native bleeding heart (*Dicentra eximia*).

Creeping phlox grows best in woodland conditions: acid soil high in organic matter. It requires ample moisture in spring, but can cope with dry soil in summer. It is hardy to Zone 4 (-30°F).

Woodland blues

Wild blue phlox (*Phlox divaricata*) is just plain gorgeous. The flowers, which open from late April through May, are lovely, in pure white or shades of blue. 'Dirigo Ice' has pale blue flowers without a trace of pink. Other selections are quite lavender or orchid in tone, and there is a white cultivar called 'Fuller's White' that contrasts vividly with surrounding foliage.

(Above) The lavender-blue flowers of wild blue phlox combine beautifully with the light green of emerging fern fronds. (Below) The cupped, heart-shaped leaves of wild ginger make an interesting and attractive alternative to English ivy.

Wild blue phlox makes a superior ground cover for shade. It grows 12 in. tall and forms large, dense drifts when it is planted in humus-rich soil under trees. Its leaves are opposite, narrow and pointed, like small, glossy green triangles all along the stems. Combine blue phlox with white trilliums, Jacob's-ladder (Polemonium reptans) or foam-flowers. Wild blue phlox is hardy to Zone 3 (-40°F)

Blue phlox spreads quite differently from the way creeping phlox spreads. New stems emerge from the base of the plant in early summer and grow until fall. The falling leaves of autumn and winter's blanket of snow flatten the stems, and the next spring, they put out roots at each leaf node (the place where the leaf emerges from the stem).

Unfortunately, rabbits enjoy the leaves of this and other phlox. The only remedy is to get rid of the bunnies or grow something else.

Gleams of white

The eastern foamflower (Tiarella cordi-folia) has everything you could want in a ground cover: evergreen, heart-shaped leaves (often with maroon veining); lovely bronze-to-burgundy winter color; and 8-in. to 12-in. tall, white, bottlebrush-like clusters of flowers in April and May. Foamflowers can thrive in dry (though not Saharan) conditions. They compete well for soil moisture and nutrients with all but the most grabby deciduous trees (Norway maples, beeches, apples) or the most dense evergreens (almost nothing grows beneath a big spruce). Foamflowers are also cold-hardy, tolerating winter lows as cold as -40°F (USDA Hardiness Zone 3).

Most foamflowers spread by sending out stolons, prostrate stems that root down at intervals. Where the stolons root, delicate pink shoots with small leaves emerge, gradually fattening to full size. A well-established plant will send out several 18-in. long stolons each year, so plants spaced on 2-ft. centers fill in rapidly.

You can also grow non-spreading foamflowers; they are appropriate for a shady border. But if you want plants that fill an area and choke out weeds, look for spreaders.

A diminutive iris

Crested iris (*Iris cristata*), a short, dense relative of more common garden irises, thrives in shade. It enjoys moist, acid soil, but even in dry shade, it spreads into carpets of stiff leaves with blue flowers that open in May along with the pure white, four-petaled flowers of the snowdrop anenome (*Anemone sylvestris*) and the azure bells of Virginia bluebells (*Mertensia virginica*). There is also a white-flowered crested iris called 'Alba' that adds a splash of light to dark corners in spring. Whatever the flower color, crested irises are extremely hardy, tolerating winter lows that can dip to -40°F (Zone 3).

Like the flowers of most irises, the blooms of the crested iris are spectacular, but fleeting. Happily, the 5-in. to 6-in. tall, dagger-shaped leaves stay an attractive, cool green throughout the whole season.

Green hearts on the march

Our native gingers are unjustly overlooked as ground covers. They resemble the more popular European ginger, but have larger leaves, often with beautiful mottling and veining. Among the natives, *Asarum canadense* is the most adaptable and readily available. It has beautifully textured, heart-shaped leaves that stand up to 8 in. tall. It spreads by sending out underground stems.

Most gardeners grow gingers for their foliage. The flowers, among the more bizarre of the plant kingdom, are brown and charming, opening from small buds to three-petaled trumpets in June. Ginger flowers don't make much of a show, but it's hard to resist stooping for a closer look.

Wild ginger thrives where moisture is abundant, but it also tolerates dry shade under trees. It grows best in a gritty soil with good drainage where winter temperatures don't drop below -30°F (Zone 4).

A spreading succulent

The tiny crowsfoot sedum (*Sedum ternatum*) delights nearly everyone who sees it. Its white, starry, triangular

The intricate blue flowers of crested irises float like butterflies above the sword-shaped, 6-in. tall leaves. Unlike bearded irises, crested irises thrive in shade.

SOURCES

The following nurseries, chosen to represent different regions in the U.S., carry at least six of the seven plants described by the author:

Busse Gardens, Rte. 2, P.O. Box 238, Cokato, MN 55321-9426, 612-286-2654. Catalog $2, deductible from first order.

The Primrose Path, R.D. 2, P.O. Box 110, Scottdale, PA 15683, 412-887-6756. Catalog $2.

Sunlight Gardens, Rte. 1, P.O. Box 600-A, Hillvale Road, Andersonville, TN 37705, 800-272-7396. Catalog $3.

Tripple Brook Farm, 37 Middle Road, Southampton, MA 01073, 413-527-4626. Catalog free.

flowers form flat heads in May, barely rising over the 2-in. to 3-in. tall, succulent, blue-green disc-shaped leaves, which remain attractive throughout the summer.

Most sedums prefer sun, but this one thrives in dry shade. In our woods, crowsfoot sedum tends to grow on neutral to alkaline soils, but it can tolerate acid soils, too. Crowsfoot sedum spreads by prostrate stems, which root where they touch the soil. It is hardy to Zone 4 (-30°F). ∎

Martha Oliver and her husband, Charles, own The Primrose Path, a nursery in Scottdale, Pennsylvania.

Three Flowers for Butterflies

Showy perennials to attract them

The orchid primrose, a striking relative of the more common ground-hugging primroses, is one of the perennials that attract the Western Tiger Swallowtail butterfly to author Yarborough's garden. Given a moist, rich soil, orchid primrose blooms for nearly a month beginning in early summer, providing plenty of nectar for butterflies.

by Alice Yarborough

There is a joy in watching big swallowtail butterflies pasturing freely among the flowers. The essence of June, however, is their odd and lovely courtship flight maneuvers: the strangely slow flutterings and almost hovering flight that mark swallowtail romance. In my first effort to attract butterflies into my garden, I sowed seeds of butterfly weed (*Asclepias tuberosa*), and I set the young plants out on a dry, sunny bank where they really took off. By the second summer, the blossoms were a luminous drift of pure orange.

Butterflies ignored them. Bumblebees were regular customers, and by late summer, bronzy, mothlike skippers were supping there, too. But the big game, the beautiful swallowtail butterflies, showed no interest. Butterfly weed was not living up to its reputation as a butterfly lure. Admittedly, my locale, western Washington, is low on resident butterfly species. Perhaps other people's butterfly weed in other sections of the country is teeming with butterflies, but mine, no.

Nevertheless, my garden, now in its fifth year, has become something of a butterfly mecca, especially during June, when elegant black-and-yellow swallowtails congregate to dine and also to court. Although I didn't originally plan the garden's site with butterflies in mind, its sunny and wind-sheltered location pleases them. My plantings offer an abundance of desirable nectar sources. (For more observations on butterflies' feeding habits, see the box on p. 69.)

On a bright June morning, perhaps nine or ten big Western Tiger Swallowtails drift in and remain in the garden for much of the day. Confronted with a considerable variety of nectar sources, they bypass all else to concentrate on three particular perennial plants. Two of their favorites are red valerian, a rosy-flowered plant familiar to many gardeners, and orchid primrose, an unusual and strikingly beautiful lilac- and crimson-flowered plant seldom encountered in American gardens. Almost as popular is Allwood's alpine pink, a low mounding plant topped with fragrant pink flowers. The red valerian and pinks are willing growers, and hardy in USDA Zones 4 through 10. The orchid primrose, considered difficult by some, can prosper for you provided its few simple needs are met. It's easy to grow from seed, and hardy in Zones 5 through 9.

I believe that the reason my garden attracts and holds butterflies is the quantity as well as the quality of nectar plants it offers. Scattered about are seven big patches of red valerian, a large group of primroses and some 20 clumps of alpine pinks. This buffet lures a number of butterfly species, but the swallowtails are undisputed winners for the title of "showiest."

Red valerian

Red valerian (*Centranthus ruber*) is available in several cultivars, ranging in color from white through shades of pink to rosy red. Seeds and plants are sold by many mail-order and local nurseries.

Seed-starting—I grew my sizable collection from seed that I started indoors. For the growing medium, I partially filled seed-starting flats with a mix of five parts garden soil to one part perlite and topped it off with an inch of sterile commercial seed-starting mix. (I use garden soil for reasons of economy, but you could just use a commercial mix.) Without the sterile mix, the seedlings would be subject to damping-off, a fungal disease that typically causes seedlings to rot near the surface of the mix, fall over and die. I sowed the seeds in the layer of sterile mix, then scattered a thin layer of the same material over them. Grown under fluorescent lights indoors, the seeds germinated in nine days, and I transplanted the seedlings to the garden five weeks later. Red valerian can be direct-sown, but in my garden, transplants compete better with the early weeds.

Bloom—Spaced 1 ft. apart, the plants grew about 2½ ft. tall and 1½ ft. in diameter. Only a few bloomed the first year, but the following summer my butterfly smorgasbord was well under way. Now flower heads made up of tiny, slightly fragrant flowers cluster on top of the stems, a lovely contrast to the gray-green leaves. Staking the plants is optional, but I usually do.

Red valerian earns its keep by blooming in my garden (USDA Zone 6) from late May almost until frost. When the first spate of blossoms is fading, around the end of June here, I deadhead the plants, cutting off each flower stalk about halfway down the stem just above a new flower-bud cluster. This task is well worth doing, as it spurs flowering for the remainder of the summer—nothing as grand as the June display, mind you, but still an attractive show. If you don't deadhead, expect to see some self-sown seedlings.

Cultural requirements—Red valerian isn't too fussy about where it grows. I set out my plants in full sun, but they tolerate partial shade. They perform well in my moisture-retentive clay loam, though I've read that they prefer excellent drainage. I don't mulch or fertilize. I water only occasionally, except in the driest weather. So far, the plants have been pest- and disease-free. In my garden, the entire top of the plants normally dies back in winter, but low shoots persist. In colder climates, I suspect that the top would die back.

Orchid primrose

The orchid primrose (*Primula vialii*) doesn't fit most people's image of a primrose. In early summer (June in my garden), it sends up a number of tallish stalks, each topped by a 5-in.- to 7-in.-long flower spike, which is densely packed with small lilac-colored bells and

This red valerian and its white-flowered cultivar are some of the swallowtail butterfly's favorite nectar plants. An easy-to-grow perennial, red valerian tolerates a wide range of conditions and blooms until frost.

tipped with the brilliant crimson calyxes of the unopened flowers. An established clump will produce a number of these strangely lovely pokers. In rich, humusy soil with ample moisture, orchid primrose often grows to roughly 1 ft. wide, and when in bloom it reaches 2 ft. tall.

Cultural requirements—A picture in the Royal Horticultural Society encyclopedia first piqued my interest in orchid primroses. Then I consulted several gardening books for cultural information. Some advised full shade; others hinted that a modest amount of sun is all to the good. I began by transplanting seven young plants in full shade and seven more in sun-dappled shade. I soon learned that the plants growing in a little sun flowered more heavily than those growing in full shade—the latter produced only a few washed-out and undersize flowers.

An accident altered my experiment and confirmed that partial sun is indeed fine. Several weeks after the orchid primroses had stopped flowering, I discovered that a mole had pushed half of them out of the ground. There they lay in the July heat, leaves wilting, with pitifully little left of their roots. Figuring that they were goners anyway, I hastily replanted what was left of them in the only empty space available, a partly sunny bed where they would receive some shade from neighboring annuals. After a good soak, the primulas never looked back. Their leaf growth was rapid and lusty. The next summer, they bloomed gorgeously. Buoyed by these results, I moved all my orchid primroses into this bed, where they bask in considerable sun during May and June and enjoy partial shade during high summer.

The plants tolerate so much sun only because my soil is heavy, moist and rich. Orchid primroses are thirsty plants, and I make sure the soil around them never begins to dry out. Gardeners with a lighter, faster-draining soil would do well to plant them in more than half-day shade and to incorporate generous amounts of humus into the soil.

Bloom—Orchid primroses usually bloom for five weeks. Their flowers are remarkably weatherproof, unfazed by the beating rains that damage other flowers. The plants seldom rebloom if they're cut back, but it's still a good idea to remove the spent flower spikes so the plant's strength

won't be shunted to seed development. Sometimes I leave a stalk or two intact and collect the ripened seeds, which produce plants identical to the parents.

Seed-starting—Orchid primroses are easy to grow from seed, though somewhat slow to germinate. Orchid primrose isn't widely available, but I've found several sources (see the box below). I sow seeds on the surface of my moist, sterile seed-starting mix in early April and set the pots on the back porch in the shade. Here in western Washington, ambient temperatures are cool enough to stratify the seeds—primulas require three weeks of prechilling, or stratification, to germinate. (You can also stratify the seeds by storing them in moist starting mix in a closed plastic bag in the refrigerator. Open the bag every second or third day for air exchange.)

Delicate, fragrant flowers covering Allwood's alpine pink, a sturdy perennial, appeal to the gardener and the tiger swallowtail alike.

My seeds germinate in about 24 days. A month later, I transplant the young plants into the garden, spacing them 1 ft. apart. Seedlings bloom the second year.

Orchid primroses die back during the winter. No top growth from the previous season remains to signal their presence. Unlike other primulas, they break dormancy very late (around May in my garden), so make sure you place a durable marker beside each plant. You'll be grateful for the marker when you're grubbing about with a weeding fork in early spring.

Division—A thriving primrose clump will need dividing probably every third year, when the plants' crowns almost push themselves above ground. The best time to divide orchid primroses is just after they've bloomed, when the old leaves are turning yellow and the new leaves are just emerging. Dig up the plant, shake the soil from its roots and gently tease the clump apart with your fingers into separate pieces with roots attached. Remove fading outer leaves and replant each piece. Keep the transplants well-watered. If they're growing in the sun, shade them for ten days or so.

Pests—I've encountered only one problem with orchid primroses. Sometimes healthy green leaves unexpectedly droop in midsummer and don't recover during the cool of the evening or when watered. When this occurs, I suspect that nemesis of primulas, the larvae of the strawberry root weevil. These tiny white grubs devour the roots, inflicting much greater damage than the adults do. (Adult weevils are small, dark beetles that chew rectangular notches in the leaves in spring and early summer.) There are several options for killing the grubs, which can be found on the outside and inside of the roots. A common recommendation is to drench the soil surrounding the plant with diazinon (1 tsp. per gallon of water), a contact insecticide, but this won't necessarily do a complete job. Another method is to apply a systemic insecticide at six-week intervals during the growing season. It will probably kill some of the larvae, but may not reach those within the main roots. As a third alternative, you can dig up the plant, thoroughly wash its roots with water, pick off any visible grubs, cut back mushy roots where the grubs have been feeding and replant the primula. This is not a task one is motivated to perform when the plant is in full bloom, so I prefer to promptly dig up affected plants after they've bloomed and inspect and wash the roots then.

For some gardeners, the orchid primrose has proved short-lived, giving rise to disgruntled cries that it must be considered a biennial. My plants are five years old, which leads me to regard this primula as a perennial when its needs are met. I'd grow it even if it didn't last as long. The combination of its exotic beauty and popularity with butterflies is enough to recommend it to me.

Allwood's alpine pink

Allwood's alpine pink (*Dianthus alpinus* 'Allwoodii', sometimes listed in catalogs as *D. Allwoodii* var. *alpinus*), the third entrée on the swallowtails' menu, is one of my favorite pinks. Its broad, low mats of silvery blue-gray foliage spill charmingly over bed edgings onto my garden paths. From May to June, the plants are covered with medium- to pale-pink, slightly fringed single flowers, many with contrasting rose or maroon eyes. The flowers are held atop 5-in.-tall sturdy stems, and send forth a light and spicy fragrance.

Cultural requirements—I started my alpine pinks from seed sown indoors in March (seed is readily available by mail-order). Lightly covered, the seeds germinated in just five days. Pinks like good drainage and sweet soil, so I worked some sand, sharp gravel and a good sprinkling of dolomite lime into my heavy, acid soil before transplanting them. In the garden, I grow them in full sun, which they require, and keep them on the dry side. After flowering, I shear off the dead heads, which stimulates rebloom throughout the rest of the summer. Most of my alpine pinks remain evergreen through the winter, but after the unusually cold winter of 1989, several clumps looked dead. I sheared them back nearly to the ground in the spring, ever hopeful. They produced a forest of new shoots, and the plants grew as beautifully as ever.

Give and take

A butterfly garden must, obviously, offer nectar plants to its beautiful visitors. If the garden is situated not too far from the caterpillar's necessary food plants, so much the better. The Western Tiger Swallowtails that grace our garden, doubtless, as voracious green caterpillars, chomp the leaves of the willows and cottonwoods so plentiful in our area. Big patches of Western bleeding-heart and numerous nettles that border our back meadow feed the caterpillars of various other butterfly species, which are valued neighbors to the flower garden. ☐

Alice Yarborough gardens in Carnation, Washington.

Illustration: Steve Buchanan

Butterflies are less flighty than they seem

by Alcinda Cundiff Lewis

A few years ago I was preparing to feed nectar to a cageful of cabbage butterflies in a ramshackle Victorian greenhouse on an English estate. The spring had been cold and damp, so there were few flowers outside, and the head gardener wouldn't let me use the prize show plants in the greenhouse for feeding butterflies. So I resorted to artificial flowers—glass tubes containing a honey and water mixture set in a platform.

To feed the butterflies, I had to put them on the platforms near the honey water, uncurl their tongues with a pin and put their tongues in the water. On the third day of performing this tedious chore, I put the "flowers" into the cage as usual. Suddenly one, then another and another butterfly flew down onto the platform and began to feed without any assistance from me! My relief at not having to hand-feed the butterflies was overshadowed by my surprise: Could the butterflies be learning to use these highly unnatural flowers? I knew that bees can learn to use artificial flowers, but they're supposed to be intelligent. Butterflies, on the other hand, are the very symbol of flightiness and frivolity. For them, learning seemed unlikely.

I didn't realize it at the time, but I had stumbled onto a way to test an explanation that Charles Darwin had proposed for a long-standing mystery in biology. In a field of many different kinds of flowers, some insects tend to visit only one species and fly over the nectar-filled flowers of other species—why is this so? This phenomenon, known as flower constancy, is clearly beneficial to the flowers, as it favors cross-fertilization within a species. But from the insects' viewpoint, it doesn't seem to make any sense. Insects waste time and energy bypassing many potential food sources.

Darwin theorized that insects remain faithful to one species because "they have just learned how to stand in the best position on the flower, and how far and in what direction to insert their proboscides [tongues]." If Darwin was right, then insects can learn how to find the nectar, but can remember how to approach only one kind of flower at a time. (If they could remember more than one flower species, there would be less need for constancy.) Darwin's hypothesis had not been fully investigated when I made my discovery. To test his theory, I decided to tackle the following questions with help from my students, assistants and family.

Are butterflies flower-constant?—To answer this question, I spent two pleasant summers following cabbage butterflies (*Pieris rapae*) in a flower-filled meadow at the New York Botanical Garden's Institute of Ecosystem Studies. I marked the flowers used by the butterflies with numbered surveyor's flags, and later went back to reconstruct the insects' flight paths. Then I compared the plant species used with the available ones, and found, contrary to previous reports, that butterflies are indeed flower-constant, although not as constant as bees. I confirmed the result of my outdoor studies with controlled greenhouse experiments.

Do butterflies learn how to find nectar in flowers?—Next I explored the butterflies' learning behavior, using greenhouse-reared, caged subjects. I watched how they approached flowers. When a butterfly first lands on a flower, it searches the sepals and petals for nectar, eventually finds it, and begins to feed. I plotted the time required for butterflies to find nectar in bellflower (*Campanula rotundifolia*) for their first eight attempts. To my surprise, they got quicker and quicker with each try, the times following a classic learning curve. I got the same results using 12 other flower species. Flighty as they seem, even butterflies can learn.

Do butterflies forget?—To test if butterflies can remember where the nectar is located in more than one type of flower at a time, I gave two groups of butterflies bellflower to learn. As soon as they had learned that, I gave the first group 20 minutes on trefoil (*Lotus corniculatus*), while the second group remained in the cage. When I retested both groups on bellflower, the first group had to relearn it, while the second group did not—learning trefoil had interfered with the former's ability to recall bellflower. Butterflies cannot remember more than one kind of flower at a time.

Rewards of learning—Darwin's hypothesis is correct, at least for the cabbage butterfly: It must learn how to extract nectar, but it cannot remember more than one species. Faithfulness to one species is time-saving behavior, allowing the insect to take advantage of the flower it already has learned rather than learning a new one. Most insects are short-lived—the cabbage butterfly, for example, lives only two weeks—so time is valuable. Time saved on feeding translates into more time for mating and reproduction. Also, if a butterfly spends less time on an exposed feeding site, it's less liable to become food for predators.

Role of flowers—To attract insects and assist them in recognizing the species they have learned, flowers have evolved distinctive combinations of colors, patterns and fragrances. All this leads to the inevitable conclusion that the beauty we work so hard to achieve in our gardens really has very little to do with us, in an evolutionary sense. But when I'm surrounded by a vibrant, sweet-scented display of flowers, I begin to doubt that it's meant only for bees and butterflies, and I wonder how Darwin would have explained human attraction to this floral advertisement. ☐

Alcinda Cundiff Lewis is a research associate in biology at the University of Colorado in Boulder.

Pale yellow flowers blanket the thread-like foliage of *Coreopsis* 'Moonbeam', billowing out to soften the front of a perennial bed. One of many long-blooming perennials, 'Moonbeam' flowers all summer and into fall.

Photo: Mark Kane

Long-Blooming Perennials
Choice plants flower at least 14 weeks

by Darrel Apps

Perennials that flower a long time make exceptionally welcome additions to the garden. With some careful selection, it's possible to have color from spring to fall, even in the summer doldrums, from just a handful of plants. The conventional wisdom is that perennials flower for about three weeks. It's not so. It's not even close. The best perennials yield at least ten weeks of bloom, and the very best flower for as long as four months.

I first realized the fallacy of the "three-week" rule when I was Departmental Head of Education at Longwood Gardens in Kennett Square, Pennsylvania. I examined bloom records collected by students on 250 species and cultivars of ornamentals. I was surprised and then delighted to find plants that bloomed as long as two or three months. I knew a list of them would be a great help to me as I designed gardens. These plants could provide a long season of color in a small space while complementing a series of other plants that might bloom at different times.

What "long-blooming" means

Quite arbitrarily, I decided that a long-blooming perennial in the mid-Atlantic states area was one that stayed in bloom for at least ten weeks, about half of the 20-22-week frost-free growing season here. There were a lot.

I'll recommend 19 of my favorites, all of which bloom for at least 14 weeks here in eastern Pennsylvania. Although length of bloom will vary

Two gold flowers spread their curving petals amid the dewy leaves and swelling buds of a 'Stella de Oro' daylily. 'Stella de Oro' has become one of the most popular daylilies in the country because it can flower for four to five months.

Photo: Mark Kane

in hotter and cooler areas, these are the longest-blooming perennials you can grow. (I'll talk about more long-bloomers in the next article [pp. 76-81]; for a complete list, see the beginning of Sources on p. 74.)

Bloom times vary, depending on climate and growing conditions. Some plants will bloom longer in the North, others for shorter periods in the South. A few will not be heat-tolerant in the Deep South. You can prolong flowering if you follow the example of the gardeners at Longwood. They do a lot of deadheading, which encourages longer bloom periods.

A blue pincushion

A few years ago in England, I saw a charming plant listed as *Scabiosa* × 'Butterfly Blue Beauty'—pincushion flower. After I got home I learned that an acquaintance had imported the plant, so we made a swap. I must say it has been one of my best trades! The cultivar name has now been shortened to 'Butterfly Blue' and trade-marked by Iverson's Perennial Gardens of Chicago. The 1½-in lavender-blue flowers start in late May and continue on until late September and some-times October. They combine nicely with the daylily 'Happy Returns' or other yellow-flowered plants such as evening primrose (*Oenothera fruticosa*). I would also recommend growing 'Butterfly Blue' in containers for a long season of color interest. Deadheading definitely improves the appearance of the 18-in. tall by 18-in. wide plants.

The plant does well in full sun and well-drained, loamy soils. Hardy to USDA Hardiness Zone 3 (-40°F), it grows south to Zone 7. It survives farther south if given light shade, but it's primarily a northern plant.

Shades of yellow

For most gardeners, green-and-gold is not a long-blooming native perennial. Usually it blooms in the spring and again in the fall. There are two forms, *Chrysogonum virginianum* var. *australe* and *C. virginianum* var. *virginianum*. The first spreads, the second forms clumps. One clump-forming culti-var, 'Mark Viette', makes a handsome, 6-in. tall plant with thick, deep green semi-evergreen leaves and perky 1-in. flowers of buttercup yellow. This one blooms off and on all summer. It should be planted on 12-in. centers for a groundcover effect. Green-and-gold grows in light shade to full sun in the North, and in the shade in the South.

The small flowers of *Scabiosa* 'Butterfly Blue' contrast pleasingly with the black-eyed Susans of *Rudbeckia* 'Goldsturm' behind them. 'Butterfly Blue' blooms from May to September if faded flowers are removed regularly.

Two long-blooming cultivars of *Coreopsis verticillata* have become very popular in the last decade. 'Moon-beam' is 18 in. tall and a pale, greenish yellow, while 'Zagreb' is shorter at 15 in. with a deep gold color. Both have daisy-like flowers about 2 in. in diameter. 'Moonbeam' starts flowering in mid-June and continues into Octo-ber. 'Zagreb' starts flowering in mid-June and usually stops a few weeks earlier than 'Moonbeam'. The foliage of 'Zagreb' is more fern-like and, in my opinion, prettier than that of 'Moon-

beam'. These two cultivars thrive from Zone 3 in Minnesota to Zone 9 in Florida and California. 'Zagreb' combines nice-ly with the blue-violet spikes of *Salvia nemorosa* 'Lubeca'. The pale yellow of 'Moonbeam' works with many colors; it's particularly nice with Russian sage. Planted on 15 in. centers, the coreop-sis quickly makes a solid ground cover.

Long bloom in the shade

For many years I admired a 6-in. tall, yellow-flowered plant with finely cut, blue-green foliage much like the leaves

Rows of small, white hearts dangle above the fern-like foliage of the bleeding-heart cultivar *Dicentra eximia* 'Alba'. The plant thrives in shade and can bloom from April to October. Wispy spires of *Calamintha nepeta* ssp. *nepeta*, a non-invasive mint relative, are just beginning to bloom behind and within the bleeding-heart.

Small, yellow, daisy-like flowers shine among the dark green leaves of *Chrysogonum virginianum*, a low-growing ground cover. The cultivar 'Mark Viette' blooms most of the summer.

stock. A mature plant reaches 15-18 in. in height. 'Alba' and 'Luxuriant' start flowering in April, and on cooler sites they continue until September and sometimes October. The flowers of 'Luxuriant' have the prettiest coloration during the cool periods of spring and fall. Both cultivars prefer bright light, but they need shade during the hottest parts of the day, growing best on deep, humus-rich soils. 'Alba' has clean white flowers over light yellow-green, fern-like foliage, while 'Luxuriant' is a deep pink in the spring and a mauve-pink during the warmer months of the summer. Its foliage is medium green. Both cultivars are hardy to Zone 3 and grow well as far south as Zone 9. In the Deep South they stop flowering during the hot summer months. In my garden these two dicentras combine well with Japanese painted ferns and *Rhododendron* 'Scintillation', which has pink flowers. Both cultivars drop spent flowers and seldom need any special attention.

A few daylilies make the grade

For years, most people thought of daylilies as easy-care, hardy, dependable plants that bloom for three weeks. Today, there are cultivars that bloom four to six weeks, and a few that bloom almost continuously. The best-known daylily that reblooms after its first flush of flowers is *Hemerocallis* 'Stella de Oro'. The 2¾-in. gold flowers, held on 1-ft. to 2-ft. scapes (flower stems), appear for 18 to 22 weeks in the mid-Atlantic states. Even the smallest division of this daylily will bloom, and clumps increase rapidly. I have seen two combinations using 'Stella de Oro' that were knockouts: at the Atlanta Botanical Garden, with *Salvia* 'May Night', which has purple flower spikes; and at North Creek Nursery here in Pennsylvania, with the new *Aster novae-angliae* 'Purple Dome', an 18-in. mound which is covered with purple, daisy-type flowers in the fall.

Daylily breeders have turned their attention to the reblooming trait and have produced a number of good cultivars with yellow or gold miniature flowers. Large-flowered reblooming daylilies in a spectrum of colors are available to gardeners in Florida and California, but not in cooler areas yet.

I started hybridizing daylilies as a hobby in 1968, and using 'Stella de Oro' as one parent, I've come up with a daylily that inherits its fine rebloom, but in a soft yellow. I call it 'Happy Returns' and find it's easy to use in

of fringed bleeding-heart, growing among the rocks at the edge of a pond at Longwood Gardens. There in the shade, *Corydalis lutea* seemed never to be out of bloom. Finally, I ordered some for the woodsy areas of my own garden where, to my amazement, it bloomed all summer, even in fairly dry shade. During July, when the weather gets hot, blooming subsides a little, but with the cooler nights of fall, flowers come back strongly. It is not easy to grow in containers, so it's scarce in garden

centers. Although it self-sows in gardens, it is difficult to grow from seed commercially. Corydalis needs shade and cool, moist soils. It does not grow well in the warmer zones.

Two other shade plants that flower for a long period are *Dicentra eximia* 'Alba' and *Dicentra* 'Luxuriant'. The fringed bleeding heart, *Dicentra eximia*, is native from New York to Georgia, and in the spring it virtually covers the floors of low, moist woodlands. Both leaves and flowers arise directly from the fragile, scaly root-

The bright pink, flat flower clusters of *Achillea millefolium* 'Fire King' mingle with salvia spires. 'Fire King' can bloom six weeks in summer and six weeks in fall.

Flat heads of dark, rosy red flowers top a young plant of *Sedum* 'Autumn Joy'. This reliable, easy-care plant first shows bright green flower buds in summer. These buds gradually turn pink, rose, rust and then brown over the course of a long season.

combinations with other plants. Other breeders are moving in the same direction. 'Lemon Lollypop' and 'Penny's Worth' are other small or miniature-sized yellows that bloom over 15 weeks each year. Other long-bloomers in gold shades are 'Forsyth Lemon Drop' and 'Yellow Lollipop', which reach 15-18 in. tall. ('Penny's Worth' is less than 12 in.

SOURCES

For a chart listing the bloom times, heights and colors of 135 long-blooming perennials, send $2 and a business-size SASE to Kerry O'Neil, Fine Gardening, P.O. Box 5506, Newtown, CT 06470-5506.

Long-blooming perennials are widely available at local garden centers and from many mail-order nurseries, large and small. The nurseries listed here carry the largest number of the plants in the story, or the ones which are more difficult to find.

The nurseries are keyed by number to the plants.

Botanical name	Sources
Achillea millefolium 'Fire King'	2,3
Aster × *frikartii* 'Monch'	1,2,4
Asteromoea mongolica	1
Chrysogonum virginianum var. *virginianum* 'Mark Viette'	4
Coreopsis verticillata 'Moonbeam'	1,2,3,4
Coreopsis verticillata 'Zagreb'	1,2,3
Corydalis lutea	3
Dicentra eximia 'Alba'	1,2
Dicentra 'Luxuriant'	1,2
Hemerocallis 'Stella de Oro'	1,4
H. 'Happy Returns'	2
H. 'Lemon Lollypop'	1
H. 'Penny's Worth'	2
Scabiosa × 'Butterfly Blue'	2,4
Sedum × 'Autumn Joy'	1,2,3*,4
Veronica longifolia 'Sunny Border Blue'	1,2,4

*Listed as 'Indian Chief'

1. **Busse Gardens**, Rte. 2, Box 238, Cokato, MN 55321-9426; 612-286-2654. Catalog $2.

2. **Carroll Gardens**, 444 East Main St., P.O. Box 310, Westminster, MD 21158. 301-848-5422. Catalog $2

3. **Lamb Nurseries**, 101 E. Sharp Ave., Spokane, WA 99202. 509-328-7956. Catalog $1.

4. **Andre Viette Farm & Nursery**, Rte. 1, Box 16, Fishersville, VA 22939. 703-943-2315. Catalog $3.

tall.) All of them grow very well in Zones 5-7 and do well in areas where there are regular summer rains.

Daylilies prefer full sun, but will grow with six hours of direct sun a day. They are heavy feeders and enjoy one or more applications of nitrogen fertilizer each season.

Lavender asters for months

If you like daisy flowers, you'll love Frikart's aster (*Aster* × *frikartii* 'Monch'). [For more on asters, including 'Monch', see *Fine Gardening* #27, pp. 26-30.] Its lavender-blue petals contrast with the yellow centers in 3-in. diameter flowers. It blooms from mid-July until October. Plants eventually reach 30 in. in height and are about 2 ft. wide. Hybridized in Switzerland about 1920, 'Monch' has gained importance in the United States only since the 1980's. I prefer its plant habit and overall performance to its sibling, 'Wonder of Staffa', which also blooms for many weeks. 'Monch' combines beautifully with the reblooming daylily 'Happy Returns'. In Zones 5 and 6 (-20°F and -10°F respectively), it needs to be mulched in winter. It grows as far south as Zone 8, and is important enough to me to be on my top-ten-perennials list.

Two old favorites

Few plants are as rewarding and dependable as *Sedum* × 'Autumn Joy'. The thick, toothed leaves provide interest all summer. The 6-in. flower heads, which start out pink and eventually turn bronze, are attractive from the end of August through October and even into November. The plant grows 24 in. tall and about 18 in. wide. A beautiful combination is 'Autumn Joy' between the foliage of *Yucca smalliana* and the soft gray carpet of *Stachys byzantina*. I also use it with the airy silver and blue Russian sage, the ornamental grasses *Miscanthus sinensis* 'Gracillimus' and *Pennisetum alopecuroides*, and with Frikart's aster.

'Autumn Joy' can be grown in full sun or bright shade over most of the United States from Zones 3-10. It prefers well-drained soil of almost any type. Tip-prune new shoots when they're 6 in. to 8 in. if they're too vigorous.

Yarrows have striking flower heads and good, ferny, gray foliage, but the blooms usually peak quickly. *Achillea millefolium* 'Fire King', when regularly deadheaded and watered, however, continues to send up flower heads most of the summer. In Longwood's perennial display, it flowers heavily from the first week of June to the middle of July, rests three to four weeks, and blooms again (somewhat sparsely) from mid-August to the end of October. I also tried four of the new German yarrow cultivars at home, but found only 'Appleblossom' bloomed as long as 'Fire King' and needed no staking. All yarrows benefit from sandy loam that's well-drained and not too fertile.

Lost plant returns

My final example of a long-blooming perennial is *Veronica longifolia* 'Sunny Border Blue'. First introduced to the trade in 1946, for a while it seemed to be lost to cultivation, but it reappeared during the last decade and has now been produced in such quantities that it is one of the most popular of all perennials. It has deep blue flower spikes that start blooming in June and continue through September. Plants grow from 24 in. to 30 in. tall. It's a good companion for yellow, pink and white-flowered plants, and is especially pretty with the pink spires of *Lythrum virgatum* 'Morden Pink' and *Hemerocallis* 'Lavender Tonic'.

'Sunny Border Blue' prefers full sun, and is tolerant of many soil types as long as they are well-drained. It grows well from Zones 4-8. Periodic deadheading improves it and probably encourages more flowering.

There is a place in the garden for more ephemeral bloomers, but selecting some of these long-blooming perennials will help you create a garden that achieves beauty and color for the whole gardening season. ■

Darrel Apps breeds and sells daylilies and designs gardens in Chadds Ford, Pennsylvania.

The flower spires of *Veronica* 'Sunny Border Blue' make a dark foil here for brilliant zinnias, achilleas and daylilies. 'Sunny Border Blue' flowers profusely for months, even in the heat of the South and the Midwest.

Photo: Renée Beaulieu

More Long-Blooming Perennials

Choice plants flower six to ten weeks

All photos, except where noted: Susan Kahn

by Darrel Apps

There is no shortage of long-blooming perennials. Like many gardeners, I used to believe that perennials bloomed for three weeks, so one key to design was choosing plants that flowered in succession. But in my own garden I've seen perennials flower for

Small, light blue flowers cling to the silver stems of Russian sage (Perovskia × superba) echoing the last purple flowers of a billowing catmint (Nepeta × faassenii). The daisy flowers of Coreopsis verticillata 'Moonbeam' glow a pale yellow while the green flowerheads of Sedum 'Autumn Joy' rise behind the catmint.

months, and my experience matched observations made by students when I worked at Longwood Gardens in Kennett Square, Pennsylvania. In the previous article (pp. 70-75), I wrote about perennials that bloom for at least 12 weeks. Here, I'll tell you about more of my favorites, long-bloomers that flower from six to ten weeks or even longer. Planting a few of them will noticeably stretch the show of color in your garden.

The dates and times given here are for Pennsylvania and the mid-Atlantic states (roughly USDA Hardiness Zone 6 [-10°F]). When and how long a plant blooms will vary according to climate and growing conditions, though, so if you live in a colder climate, your plants may well bloom later; in a warmer climate, they may bloom earlier. It's more difficult to predict how their length of bloom will vary—try them and find out.

Daisies all summer

I've always been an admirer of single daisy flowers, and one of my favorites is the Korean chrysanthemum, *Chrysanthemum × rubellum* 'Clara Curtis'. (The genus has recently been reclassified as *Dendranthema rubella*.) I have vivid memories of it in my first garden, 25 years ago in Wisconsin. The 2½-in. wide daisies start out deep pink, then fade to softer shades. In Pennsylvania, 'Clara Curtis' usually starts blooming as early as mid-July and continues off and on until late September. With a little deadheading, the effective period of bloom is just over ten weeks. 'Clara Curtis' makes a pretty combination with *Artemisia* 'Silver King' and Frikart's aster.

'Clara Curtis' is winter-hardy to Zone 4 (-30°F) and grows as far south as Zone 9. It prefers full sun, and usually grows less than 2 ft. tall and spreads to about 18 in. In fertile soils, 'Clara Curtis', like many chrysanthemums, will soon become crowded. When it does, divide the plants, and they'll do much better.

Another daisy-like flower is gaillardia. A friend of mine once called it "glare of the garden," but its bright, two-toned flowers can be combined with other plants, and it blooms almost constantly from late May to September. One of the best cultivars is *Gaillardia × grandiflora* 'Baby Cole'. Growing only 8 in. tall, it produces big (2-in. to 3-in. diameter) daisies whose yellow petals are edged in burgundy. 'Baby Cole' and the daylily 'Thumbelina' combine nicely in the foreground of a bed.

Gaillardia is hardy to Zone 2 (-50°F) and extremely heat-tolerant, but often short-lived. You can grow plants as annuals or you can improve their longevity by fall root-pruning. Just drive a shovel into the ground around the plant to sever its roots to initiate vigorous new growth before frost. Often the severed roots send up shoots, and these new plants will over-winter even though the parent plant dies.

Spiky flowers that last

The purple loosestrife *Lythrum virgatum* 'Morden Pink' makes a beautiful display. Its rosy mauve flower spikes, the size of bottlebrushes, rise to 5 ft. or more for ten weeks (and sometimes longer) from June to August. A handsome combination used at Longwood Gardens when I worked there was 'Morden Pink' with the daylilies 'Perennial Pleasure' and 'Prairie Blue Eyes'.

Adapted in Zones 3 (-40°F) through 9, 'Morden Pink' prefers full sun and is most successful when it has ample water. Loosestrife also tolerates a wide range of soil types and moisture conditions, from well-aerated, sandy soils to soggy bottom lands. Some years Japanese beetles have eaten the flowers in my garden.

Unfortunately, loosestrife can be hazardous. A close relative, *Lythrum salicaria*, is an invasive nuisance, outlawed in several states because it destroys wetland plant ecology. 'Morden Pink' is self-sterile, but it will set seeds if there are other loosestrife species nearby, so it still isn't permitted in some areas. (Washington State prohibits importation of any loosestrifes.)

A relatively new selection of catmint, *Nepeta × faassenii* 'Dropmore', is a beautiful plant for edging garden beds or paths, a fine companion for hybrid tea roses and a perfect choice for herb gardens (see photo at left). Spikes of mauve-purple flowers appear in May and usually repeat, though somewhat sparsely, until September. (I cut mine back hard before bloom in late spring so they'll flower heavily during daylily season.) The flowers rest on beautiful, silver-gray foliage, making a mound about 18 in.

True blue flowers bloom on the low-growing plumbago *Ceratostigma plumbaginoides.* Growing between paving stones, the plumbago complements the orange flowers of butterfly weed. Plumbago emerges very late in the spring, but makes up for the delay with six weeks of bloom in late summer and early fall.

to 24 in. tall and nearly as wide. The foliage is fragrant when bruised or crushed. Hardy to Zone 4, *N.* × *faassenii* prefers full sun. Cats do, indeed, love it—I have to place strategic stakes to keep my cat from flattening it.

Russian sage (*Perovskia* × *atriplicifolia* , now renamed *P.* × *superba*) is another good plant for full sun. Long, thin spikes of light blue flowers rise above silver-blue, serrated leaves to a height of about 40 in. Flowers persist for up to 15 weeks. Old flowers drop off before they look bad, so the plants always seem perky and fresh, even without deadheading. Russian sage combines well with white and yellow flowers; I like it with the white 'Mt. Fuji' summer phlox, which is about the same height, or with the yellow-green flowers of *Coreopsis verticillata* 'Moonbeam' (see photo on p. 76).

Native from Afghanistan to Tibet, Russian sage can withstand severe summer heat and grows well from Zones 3 through 9. It is deep-rooting and prefers well-drained soils, doing best on sandy soils. *P. atriplicifolia* tends to flop as it matures; *P.* × 'Longin', which is beginning to appear in catalogs, has a more upright habit.

If you'd like months of striking indigo-blue flowers, try *Salvia* × *sylves-tris* 'May Night' (see photo on opposite page). Each stem produces several flower spikes swaying 18 in. to 24 in. high. 'May Night' starts flowering in mid-May and continues on and off until frosts in the fall. Periodic dead-heading encourages rebloom. It prefers well-drained soils and full sunlight. Hardy to Zone 4, it doesn't do well in the hot climates of the Deep South (Zone 8). Slugs love it; if they thrive in your garden, 'May Night' won't. It makes a good companion for *Coreopsis auriculata* 'Nana' in early summer.

Enduring coneflowers

Among black-eyed Susans, one of the most popular is the orange coneflower, *Rudbeckia fulgida* var. *sullivantii* 'Goldsturm'. Although it doesn't actually bloom all summer, as some gardeners claim, it does brighten things up for seven or eight weeks, starting in mid-July. Plants form large clumps of deep green basal leaves. The flowers, brassy orange rays surrounding a brown cone, sit atop stems 18 in. to 30 in. high and combine nicely with blue flowers such as Russian sage or the annual *Salvia farinacea* 'Victoria'. Easy to grow in most areas of the country (Zones 3 to 9), *R. fulgida* can become a self-seed-ing, weedy pest in cultivated soils.

If you have a large garden, you should try the cut-leaved coneflower, *R. nitida*. Its slightly droopy, sulphur yellow flowers can reach heights of 5 ft. or more. The cultivar 'Autumn Glory' grew 6 ft. tall at Longwood Gardens and flowered from late July to September. 'Golden Glow' is just as tall and double-flowered; 'Autumn Sun' (also called 'Herbstonne') looks like 'Autumn Glory' but is 4 ft. to 5 ft. tall. Combined with Russian sage and the goldenrod 'Peter Pan', it's quite stunning. If you need a smaller plant, try the shorter, double 'Goldquelle', which reaches 3 ft. but needs deadheading to look neat. All rudbeckias perform well in Zones 4 through 10.

Purple coneflowers, American natives of the genus *Echinacea*, are equally at home in formal borders or wildflower gardens. Of the many cultivars of *Echinacea purpurea*, 'Bright Star' (see photo on opposite page) and 'Magnus' are among the best. Their distinctive, slightly drooping, bold pink flowers appear atop 2-ft. to 3-ft. stems in mid-June and continue on to the end of July, easily six weeks. The coarse, dark green leaves are attractive before the plants bloom. For a few years, one of the best combinations in my borders was 'Magnus' with

Acanthus mollis, Nepeta × *faassenii* and the daylily 'Yesterday Memories'. Purple coneflowers can be grown in regular garden soils and full sun from Zones 3 through 8.

A new tall plant

If you want the drama of a tall perennial, try *Patrinia scabiosifolia* (see photo p. 81). I first saw it in 1984, while collecting plants in Korea for Longwood Gardens and the U.S. National Arboretum. The patrinias there grew about 3 ft. to 4 ft. tall and varied in form from branched to nearly unbranched. They reminded me of the dill that my mother planted for pickling cucumbers. I grew several patrinia plants from seeds collected later that year and was surprised to find, when they flowered the following fall, that they topped out at 7 ft. tall. Masses of tiny yellow flowers appeared in August and continued on until October. I moved them with a clump of soil the following spring to combine with the big ornamental grass *Miscanthus sinensis* 'Strictus' and a deciduous holly with bright berries, *Ilex verticillata* 'Winter Red'.

While I was in Korea, I noticed that patrinias were often used as cut flowers and displayed with red pepper fruit in beautiful vases. Inspired, I cut some patrinia flowers for the house, where I was horrified to find out they had an incredible "wet dog" smell!

I'm not absolutely sure of the winter-hardiness of *P. scabiosifolia*, but I would

Spikes of dark blue flowers rise from the crowns of *Salvia* x *sylvestris* '**May Night**'. If spent flowers are removed regularly, the 18-in. to 24-in. flower stems may repeat, off and on, from May to frost.

guess that it will grow from Zones 6 to 9. My first plants survived three seasons and then succumbed, but I replaced them easily with seedlings that had come up nearby.

I have also learned that there are other patrinias grown in American gardens. *P. gibbosa*, a species that flowers earlier, is a much shorter perennial and looks something like a large lady's-mantle plant.

A ground cover for late-summer bloom

During the heat of summer, blue is a soothing relief to the pervasiveness of hot-colored flowering plants. I've always enjoyed the deep blue color of the plumbago *Ceratostigma plumbaginoides* (see photo on opposite page). Its bloom time here in the mid-Atlantic states is from mid-August through September. When the blooms first appear, the foliage is green, but by the end of the bloom cycle, the leaves start turning plum shades. It grows 15 in. tall and spreads to make a solid mat. Leaves are slow to emerge in the spring. It is hardy in Zone 5 (-20°F) and grows as far south as Zone 9.

I've used plumbago successfully with *Coreopsis verticillata* 'Zagreb', *Helianthus* × *multiflorus* 'Flore-Pleno', *Hemerocallis* 'Stella de Oro' and *Rudbeckia fulgida* var *sullivantii*. I have also seen it used successfully as a ground cover under *Prunus cerasifera* 'Thundercloud'. The spent, violet-

The thistle-like foliage and perfectly spherical blue flowers of *Echinops ritro* contrast with the drooping, bold pink ray flowers of the purple coneflower, *Echinacea purpurea* 'Bright Star'. Both plants are reliably hardy to USDA Hardiness Zone 3 (-40°F) and bloom in midsummer.

Photo: top, Chris Curless

Yellow and green throats accent the bold red flowers of *Hemerocallis* 'Pardon Me', a daylily that is short of stature but long on bloom. 'Pardon Me' is one of the recent daylily introductions which flowers reliably for about six weeks in midsummer, about twice as long as the traditional bloom period for these care-free perennials.

Golds feature 'Camden Gold Dollar', 'Condilla', and 'Jen Melon'. Among the pinks you'll find 'Pink Corduroy', 'Pink Recurrence' and 'Vi Simmons'. Finally there is the near-white 'Joan Senior'. These and many more can be found in specialist daylily catalogs.

Another tried and true garden performer is the yarrow *Achillea* × 'Coronation Gold' (see lower photo on opposite page). Dense, flat clusters of tiny, yellow-gold flowers appear above fern-like gray foliage for six weeks starting in the first part of June in the mid-Atlantic states. Its bloom time overlaps with lavender 'Munstead', true lilies, loosestrifes, catmints, salvias and several veronicas, and it combines nicely with all of them. Fall flower arrangements often include the dried flower heads of 'Coronation Gold'. Hardy to Zone 3, it enjoys hot, full sun and well-drained soils.

The old-fashioned red valerian (*Centranthus ruber* 'Roseus', sometimes listed as *C.r.* var. *roseus*) is too often overlooked today. It bears dense terminal clusters of small, pink-red flowers above blue-green foliage that is 18 in. to 24 in. high and about as wide. The first summer I grew 'Roseus', it bloomed for six weeks starting in mid-May and then bloomed again in August. The flowers easily clash with other pinks, so it's best to grow it as a specimen surrounded by green-leaved plants. I have also seen it combined attractively with *Achillea* × 'Moonshine'.

Red valerian is hardy in Zone 5, and it thrives on rather hot and dry, well-drained sites. It also tolerates limey soils. In surviving Renaissance gardens in Italy, red valerian commonly grows in the lime-mortar joints of walks and walls.

Expanding your plant palette

The long-blooming perennials I've described here and on pp. 70-75 provide a rich palette of color. Flowering for weeks, even months, they can enliven your garden from spring to fall. But grow the three-week perennials, too. After all, the ephemeral nature of some plants is what makes gardening an adventure. I know a gardener who invites friends to watch his evening primroses open. The show is over in 15 minutes, but they all get a kick out of it. □

Darrel Apps breeds and sells daylilies and designs gardens in Chadds Ford, Pennsylvania.

colored flower heads complement the leaves in a pleasant textural contrast.

Plumbago can be used generously near the front of a border. It is somewhat invasive, but that is its real virtue. Each spring you may want to dig out last year's increase and get the plant back to home base.

Old favorites

An old standby in perennial borders is garden phlox, *Phlox paniculata*. Of the numerous cultivars of this species, I have grown three that bloom for over ten weeks from July to September. 'Eva Cullum' (see photo on opposite page) offers rose-pink flowers, 'Franz Schubert' is lilac with a darker eye, and 'Sandra' has very bright orange-red flowers. All grow 2½ ft. to 3 ft. tall ('Sandra' is usually shortest) and are hardy in Zone 4. I like 'Franz Schubert' with the daylily 'Joan Senior' and *Artemisia* 'Silver King'. Deadheading lengthens the flowering season and eliminates seedlings, which are likely to lose the traits of the cultivars.

Many gardeners have given up on garden phlox because of the species' susceptibility to powdery mildew, which makes the plants unsightly although it usually doesn't kill them. I've found that good cultural practices can greatly reduce the problem. In the spring, when new shoots in a clump reach 8 in. to 10 in. tall, cut to the ground all but four or five well-spaced, healthy ones to allow good air circulation. It also helps to dig up a clump every two or three years and replant only the most vigorous shoots.

Extending the season of bloom is a goal of many daylily (*Hemerocallis*) hybridizers. On p. 73, I suggested several that bloom or rebloom over a period of 14 weeks or more. A group of recent introductions blooms or reblooms for six weeks or more. Yellow-flowered cultivars include 'Brocaded Gown', 'Green Flutter', 'Jakarta', 'Golden Fountain', 'Offa' and 'Sounds of Silence'. Reds include 'Oriental Ruby', 'Pardon Me' (see photo above), 'Red Rum', 'Scarlet Orbit' and 'Woodside Fire Dance'.

The rose-pink flowers of *Phlox paniculata* 'Eva Cullum' top 30-in. stems. Deadheading encourages bloom, and thinning stems in the spring helps reduce mildew problems.

SOURCES

For a chart listing the bloom times, heights and colors of 135 long-blooming perennials, send $2 (payable to Fine Gardening) and a business-sized SASE to Ms. Kerry O'Neil, Fine Gardening, P.O. Box 5506, Newtown, CT 06470-5506.

These mail-order sources offer the widest selection or the hardest-to-find of the long-blooming perennials mentioned by the author:

Carroll Gardens, 444 E. Main St., P.O. Box 310, Westminster, MD 21157. 301-848-5422. Catalog $2. Lists 14 perennials and 2 daylilies.

Holbrook Farm, 115 Lance Rd., P.O. Box 368, Fletcher, NC 28732-0368, 704-891-7790. Catalog free. Lists 5 perennials, including *Patrinia scabiosifolia,* and 1 daylily.

Wayside Gardens, Hodges, SC 29695. 800-845-1124. Catalog free. Lists 14 perennials, including *Phlox paniculata* 'Eva Cullum' and 'Sandra'.

For the long-blooming daylilies mentioned:

Big Tree Daylily Garden, 777 General Hutchinson Parkway, Longwood, FL 32750-3705. 407-831-5430. Catalog $1, refundable. Lists 11 daylilies.

Soules Garden, 5809 Rahke Rd., Indianapolis, IN 46217. 317-786-7839. Dec.1 - March 10: 4421 Lane Rd., Zephyrhills, FL 33541. 813-783-3616. Catalog $1, refundable. Min. order $10. Lists 8 daylilies, including *Hemerocallis* 'Jakarta'.

Woodside Gardens, 824 Williams Lane, Chadds Ford, PA 19317, 215-388-6901. Catalog $2. Lists 7 daylilies, including *Hemerocallis* 'Sounds of Silence' and 'Woodside Fire Dance'.

Two long-blooming perennials fill out this quartet. Flat heads of gold flowers top the silver-gray foliage of an old standby, *Achillea* x 'Coronation Gold'. In late summer, sprays of tiny, pale yellow flowers branch from the tall stems of *Patrinia scabiosifolia* in the background, complementing the briefer appearance of the yellow daylily *Hemerocallis* 'Erin Prairie'. Graceful sprays of the ornamental grass *Pennisetum alopecuroides* round out the planting.

Annual Charmers

Their wealth of color refreshes the perennial garden

The lavender flowers of tall verbena float on thin, branching stems that allow a clear view of red cannas behind. Verbena is one of many long-flowering annuals that enhance perennial plantings. Feathery red heads of celosia punctuate the foreground.

Photo: Susan Kahn

by Rob Proctor

In my mixed garden borders, annuals, bulbs, perennials and shrubs mingle with abandon. The perennials and shrubs form the backbone; annuals and bulbs provide the sparks that keep me excited throughout the season. As one perennial fades and another comes into its own, annuals smooth the transition.

To fit in with the informal borders around my 1896 cottage, the annuals I grow must display an uninhibited charm. My garden overflows with old-fashioned favorites that I write about as well as new introductions that I evaluate. I look for annuals whose grace and refinement blend in well with the willowy perennials and exuberant shrubs that are a part of my mixed plantings.

The annuals I grow serve as more than mere filler for a border. They tie together clumps of perennials and shrubs. They obscure the shortcomings (the "gangly legs" or stiff posture) of some otherwise-desirable perennials. They conceal the dying foliage of spring bulbs and fill the gaps left behind when the bulb leaves wither. Finally, annuals echo and complement nearby container plantings.

There are many annuals whose character makes them well-suited for mixed plantings. Some of my favorites, such as sunflowers, calendula and borage, have been grown for centuries. Others, such as heliotrope, mealy-cup sage and creeping zinnia, were favorites of the Victorians, who went through a craze of growing bedding plants—short-growing annuals in riotous colors—in designs that resembled Oriental carpets. Compared to typical bedding plants, the annuals I prefer offer a greater diversity of shapes, sizes and flowering habits. Their colors are often less strident, making them easier to incorporate into a mixed border. The gardener who discovers the joy of these annuals will find limitless possibilities. Combinations are endless, and the selection is nearly so. Annuals are less expensive than perennials, so you can affordably change color schemes and combinations yearly, as well as repeat successful ones.

You won't usually see the annuals I favor displayed in garden centers alongside gaudy-colored, squat marigolds, salvias or petunias. But you can easily grow these uncommon annuals from seed, which is readily available by mail-order (see Sources, p. 87).

Tall stars for the back of the border

Annuals are often stars in their own right. One of my favorite tall annuals is tall verbena *(Verbena bonariensis)*. This plant behaves as a perennial in climates milder than mine (USDA Hardiness Zone 5 [-20°F]), but its annual habit here does not dissuade me from growing it each year. Its sprays of tiny, rosy lavender blooms, which grow on thin, straight, 5-ft. tall stems, open in midsummer and continue until frost. This froth of lavender provides continuity as other flowers come and go. Like a good party host, it doesn't dominate, but brings out the best in its companions. The stems take up very little space, so verbena can be planted within inches of perennials. And because it's a see-through plant, it never obscures nearby plants, it highlights

A cleome, or spider flower, clusters dozens of pink blooms and wiry pistils (reproductive parts) atop a single upright stem. Cleomes bloom all summer.

Photo: Chris Curless

them. It is the best of companions for tall lilies, sunflowers or phlox.

Other back-of-the border annuals command attention with their tall, architectural structure. Stately castor bean (*Ricinus communis*), with its broad, deeply-lobed, dark green or bronze leaves, grows 4 ft. to 20 ft. tall, and bears spiny, red seed pods. (Seeds of castor bean are deadly poisonous if ingested.) Spider flower (*Cleome hasslerana*) bears large, delicate pink or white flowers atop prickly, 5-ft. tall stems (see photo on p. 83). Woodland tobacco (*Nicotiana sylvestris*) sports a candelabra of tubular, night-scented flowers on stems up to 5 ft. tall. They rise over bright green, basal leaves that form a yard-wide rosette.

I prefer to plant tall annuals at the back of a border, where their bold foliage or unusual flowers complement or contrast with tall perennials. Planted in repeating groups, the tall annuals unify their companions.

Mid-border annuals

There are many mid-height annuals that can contribute loads of flowers in the middle of the border without sacrificing a wildflower-like grace and form. There's no question about my mid-border favorites—rose mallow (*Lavatera trimestris*) and cheese mallow (*Malva sylvestris*). They bloom with abandon. I never tire of their silky, simple blossoms. Rose mallow usually grows to 3 ft. tall and produces a pro-

The simple, satiny pink flowers of rose mallow reach out from the top of 3-ft. tall stems from June until frost.

fusion of 2½-in. wide pink or white blooms, usually from June until frost. Cheese mallow grows 2 ft. tall or more. It, too, begins to bloom in June. Its five-petaled, 2-in. wide, lavender-pink flowers are marked with prominent violet stripes.

Mallows tend to go to seed halfway through the summer, which stops their flowering. To promote more flowering, I cut many of my plants back to 6 in. before they form seeds. New stems grow, and in about three weeks, they start flowering again and continue until frost. To prevent a hacked up look, I cut back just a few at a time.

You might consider other annuals that grow between 2 ft. and 4 ft. tall for the middle of the border. Plants with spikes of flowers can add important vertical accents to beds where round plants predominate. Larkspur (*Consolida* spp.) has spikes with blue or pink blossoms, mealy-cup sage (*Salvia farinacea*) features spires of blue or white, and lemon mint (*Monarda citriodora*) bears mauve-pink tiers of blossoms. Tickseed (*Coreopsis tinctoria*) produces bright gold or reddish flowers on thin, airy stems from July until frost if you periodically remove its spent blossoms.

On the edge

Low-growing annuals also find a place in a mixed border. I edge beds and walks with old favorites like sweet alyssum, which has tiny, airy flowers of white, rose or lavender; creeping zinnia (*Sanvitalia procumbens*), a spreading mound of tiny, dark-eyed yellow daisies; and classic zinnia (*Zinnia angustifolia*), a tireless producer of masses of single, daisy-like blossoms in brilliant golden orange or pristine white. All three bloom prolifically from June until frost, hold up well in heat and stay under 6 in. in height. By planting them in drifts that extend into the border and mingle with other plants, I disguise the seams of the garden.

The ferny young seedlings of love-in-a-mist (*Nigella damascena*), another edging annual, quickly produce 1-in. wide, sky-blue, deeper blue, pale cranberry or white flowers enclosed by a puff of lacy leaves. The flowers are followed by bloated, spiky seed pods that are pretty in dried bouquets.

Self-sowing volunteers

I especially admire annuals that make themselves at home and return year after year on their own. If I let them go to seed, nearly all the annuals in my

In a container combination, the pure white of classic zinnia intensifies the colors of other annuals, including red nicotiana, pink dianthus, golden nasturtium and silvery-leaved dusty miller. This low-growing zinnia can also brighten edges of beds and borders.

Photos: top, Rob Proctor; bottom, Nancy Beaubaire

mixed borders self-sow—the seeds over-winter safely and germinate in spring, giving me a crop of volunteer seedlings. Volunteers give the garden an atmosphere of carefree informality and fullness. Some of my favorites are orange-flowered California poppies; white, pink or rose cosmos (see photo on p. 86); blue bachelor's-buttons; orange and yellow calendulas; purple and yellow Johnny-jump-ups, with their small, pansy-like flowers; and signet marigolds, small, mounding plants whose lacy foliage is smothered with gold, orange or yellow flowers.

Another self-sower I find invaluable is borage (Borago officinalis), which grows to about 2 ft. and blooms from June to October. Although it cannot compete with the fireworks of showier, brighter flowers, I am pleased by its true-blue star flowers and hairy, silvery leaves. I especially like borage combined with 'Sonata' cosmos, a 2-ft. tall plant with pink or white flowers.

Amazingly enough, volunteers tend to stay in the part of the garden to which they are best suited. But giant self-sowers sometimes invade the front of the border. Occasionally, I let a tall cosmos cultivar stay near the front just for fun, but otherwise I remove the seedlings of big self-sowers.

Fragrance

While a garden is largely for visual delight, it should contain scented plants, too. When an annual possesses good looks, easy culture and fragrance, it becomes especially valuable. I allow the most room for old-fashioned flowering tobacco (Nicotiana alata), which grows 3 ft. to 4 ft. tall. The evening breeze in July and August is laden with the sweet fragrance of its white, star-shaped blossoms. I also rely on its shorter hybrid offspring, such as the 'Domino', 'Nicki' and 'Starship' series, which grow from 12 in. to 20 in. tall. While they have just a light fragrance, their short stature makes them the best replacements for faded tulips and daffodils. They bloom prolifically throughout summer and autumn in clear colors of pink, rose-red, white and chartreuse. I especially favor the chartreuse flowers of 'Nicki Lime', 'Nicki Yellow' or 'Starship Lemonlime.' They are a pretty complement for many perennials and shrubs, such as pink mallow (Malva alcea 'Fastigiata'), peach-colored daylilies or hydrangea 'Annabelle', whose blooms open white and change to pale green.

The blue flowers and airy foliage of love-in-a-mist create a delicate edge for this planting of vibrant pink Silene hookeri and purple and blue Delphinium ajacis.

For fragrance, I also like to plant stock (Matthiola incana), night-scented stock (Matthiola bicornis) and heliotrope (Heliotropium arborescens). They all perfume the garden and mix in with other plants effortlessly. I prefer the smaller types of stock, 1 ft. tall or less, because they are easier to position.

Their dense, conical flower heads range from white to pale pink to lavender and rose-violet. They all carry a spicy clove scent, stronger than carnations. Night-scented stock, a ground-hugging plant, opens at dusk. Its four-petaled lavender blossoms release a sweet, intoxicating perfume that can be

Gleaming white flowers highlight the feathery foliage of cosmos, an easy-to-grow, self-sowing annual. Cosmos cultivars range in height from 2 ft. to 3 ft. tall.

shapes. Clumps of dusty miller (*Senecio cineraria*), with its finely cut, silvery leaves, grow 10 in. tall and shine in sun or part shade. [For more on dusty miller, see the article on pp. 8-11.] Polka dot plant (*Hypoestes phyllostachya*) is aptly named for the splattering of pink, white or red spots on its deep green or bronze leaves. If you keep it compact (under 8 in. tall) by periodically pinching back the foliage, polka dot plant will sparkle in shady combinations with impatiens and ferns. Coleus hybrids, which I also pinch for compactness, come in so many leaf shades and patterns that they have great possibilities for shady beds or for sunny beds that receive abundant moisture. Planted near the front of the border, just behind edging plants, the deep red coleus varieties underscore the silver-edged leaves and white flowers of dead nettle (*Lamium* 'White Nancy') in shade, while chartreuse coleus pairs prettily with the silver leaves of lamb's-ears in more sun.

Deep purple-leaved Chinese basil (*Perilla frutescens*) sets off pink or red flowers in the garden and contrasts beautifully with silver-leaved plants. It closely resembles its relative, coleus, but distinguishes itself with the metallic sheen of its leaves. Chinese basil grows 15 in. to 30 in. tall in sun or light shade, but may be kept more compact with pinching. Its flowers are insignificant, but I allow a few to remain on the plant so it can self-sow.

I also value bronze fennel and dill for their foliage, though they are most often grown only in the herb or vegetable patch. Their refined, feathery foliage makes a striking contrast planted behind bee balm (a perennial with pink, red or purple flowers) or with summer-blooming bulbs like lilies or cannas.

Getting started

Most of the annuals I've mentioned are easy to grow from seed. Garden centers sell plants of some of them, but only mail-order seed suppliers have all of them.

There is no secret to mixing annuals with perennials, shrubs and bulbs in the garden. Most annuals are shallow-rooted, so they can comfortably share space with other plants. After bulbs have bloomed, pull the foliage aside and slide annual seedlings gently into place. The bulb foliage will shade the young plants until they can take over. Even thick ground covers can be

discerned 20 ft. away. Heliotrope may grow 2 ft. tall or more, but dwarf varieties reach only half that height. Clusters of tiny purple flowers top deep green foliage. Not all seedlings carry heliotrope's fabled "cherry pie" fragrance, so many gardeners overwinter their best plants indoors or propagate new plants from cuttings of highly-scented cultivars such as 'Iowa'.

Annuals for foliage

Bloom and fragrance aside, I grow many annuals for their leaf colors and carefully pulled aside to insert annuals. However, ground covers make ideal hangouts for slugs and cutworms, so I'm especially vigilant about controlling them until the seedlings establish themselves. Self-sowers are the easiest. Once you've planted them, let them go to seed. Thin the seedlings, removing unwanted ones or transplanting extras to other areas of the garden.

In my garden, I have a "no-bare-earth" policy—bare spots get filled with something as soon as possible. This approach results in on-the-spot design decisions, but since I prefer pastel flowers and silver and bronze leaves, most plants that I add are compatible with those already in place. Fortunately, there are plenty of annuals that fit the bill. I finish the bulk of planting by the middle of June, but I continue to visit nurseries and to trade with friends throughout the summer looking for any possible new additions. The pleasure of gardening in this manner, for me, is in sharing my favorites and acquiring new plants that will find a permanent spot in my garden. □

Rob Proctor is a botanical illustrator, an instructor at Denver Botanic Gardens and an author whose books include Annuals, Perennials and Country Flowers.

SOURCES

Seeds for annuals are widely available from many mail-order nurseries. Those listed here carry the largest number of annuals mentioned by the author, or those that are more difficult to locate.

W. Atlee Burpee & Co., Warminster, PA 18974; 800-888-1447. Catalog free.

The Country Garden, P.O. Box 3539, Oakland, CA 94609; 510-658-8777. Catalog $2.

The Fragrant Path, P.O. Box 328, Fort Calhoun, NE 68023. Catalog $1.

Pinetree Garden Seeds, New Gloucester, ME 04260; 207-926-3400. Catalog free.

Plants of the Southwest, Rte. 6, Box 11A, Sante Fe, NM 87501; 505-471-2212. Catalog with 113 color photos, $3.50; listing of offerings, free.

Shepherd's Garden Seeds, 30 Irene Street, Torrington, CT 06790; 203-482-3638. Catalog $1.

Stokes Seeds Inc., P.O. Box 548, Buffalo, NY 14240; 800-263-7233. Catalog free.

Thompson & Morgan, Inc., P.O. Box 1308, Jackson, NJ 08527; 201-363-2225. Catalog free.

The deep purple leaves of Chinese basil, an annual grown for its striking foliage, provide a rich contrast to the perennials in this border. Delicate pink anemone flowers top slender stems in the foreground, the salmon flower heads of sedum 'Autumn Joy' are tucked below to the right, and the grassy, green and white leaves of variegated miscanthus drape gracefully behind.

Purple heliotrope flowers cluster above deep green leaves. Heliotropes, which grow 1 ft. to 2 ft. tall or more, scent the garden with a sweet perfume reminiscent of cherry pie.

Annual Vines

Quick climbers offer flowers till frost

by Gary Keim

Annual vines are among the most rewarding of garden plants. They are easily started from seed, fast-growing and undemanding, and best of all, they flower profusely for an exceptionally long time. What's more, by standing in for perennial vines, annual vines can help you figure out the best place for their perennial cousins. The old adage about perennial vines says, "The first year they sleep, the second year they creep, and the third year they leap." From a gardener's point of view, three years can be a frustratingly long wait for a vine to get up and running. If you'd rather see quicker results, and if you enjoy experimenting with interesting plants, try annual vines.

Annual vines are versatile plants. Their wide range of foliage textures and flower colors offers choices that complement every garden style. The plants are especially suited to small gardens, where there's rarely room to spread outward, but always room to reach upward. Fences, walls, arbors or even the airspace above beds and borders can provide annual vines with a home. Annual vines can enhance garden features or be spectacular focal points. Flanking a path, they create a welcoming passageway where the blossoms (and fragrance) can be readily enjoyed up close. Even a single vine placed in a key position makes an impact, adding height to a garden, softening the hard lines of permanent features and quickly masking eyesores.

Most annual vines bloom profusely in summer when many other plants flag from the heat. When you grow annual vines, your summer garden attracts butterflies, bees and hummingbirds with an attractive food source.

I'll tell you about nine annual vines that I've grown here in northwestern Connecticut and recommend highly. They should perform equally well and be as easy to grow in the rest of the U.S. I urge you to try others on your own; an enormous number of annual vines are just waiting to be discovered.

Hyacinth bean—One of the most sought-after annual vines of recent years is a dazzling twiner from the vegetable gardens of the Orient. Hyacinth bean (*Dolichos lablab*, also known as *Lablab purpurea*), a member of the pea and bean family, is a marvelous study in purple. Its stems and flower buds are beet purple, its compound leaves are purplish-green, and its ½-in. flowers, clustered on upright spikes, are purple-pink and white. The real surprise is its flat, deep purple pods, which add greatly to the vine's decorative qualities, as if it needed anything else. This spectacular vine never fails to attract comment. Hyacinth bean also comes in a white-flowered form, which I've never grown, and a green-leaved form with light purple blossoms that isn't nearly as showy. A heat-lover, hyacinth bean should be transplanted into the garden only after the soil is thoroughly warmed.

Asarina—Creeping gloxinia (*Asarina erubescens*) and the kindred *A. scandens*, members of the figwort family, originated in Mexico. (See photos on p. 90.) *A. erubescens* has soft, gray-green, triangular leaves, 2 in. to 3 in.

long, and solitary, 3-in. diameter, rosy-pink trumpets. It blooms from mid- to late summer until frost. A daintier plant, *A. scandens* has shiny, dark green, ¾-in. long leaves and ½-in. bluish-purple flowers not unlike those of snapdragons. What *A. scandens* lacks in bloom size it compensates for with an inordinate number of blossoms. From the time plants are only a foot tall in late spring, the show is nonstop until hard frost.

Several years ago, my plants rambled through a young rose-of-Sharon shrub, and the next summer, self-sown seedlings created a repeat performance. An inverted tomato cage has also proven to be a suitable support. Both asarina species grow nicely in pots if the pots are at least 12 in. in diameter. Both species are also very fast growing, reaching 8 ft. to 10 ft. by season's end. They climb by petioles—leaf stems that wrap around objects for support. (See "How Vines Climb," pp. 90-91, for more on this subject.)

Cup-and-saucer vine—If you're looking for a workhorse to cover a large area or hide an unsightly view, then cup-and-saucer vine (*Cobaea scandens*) is for you. (See photo on p. 91.) This member of the phlox family, native to Mexico, has the intriguing habit of climbing by tendrils borne at the ends of its leaves. In midsummer, single, greenish-purple, violet or white flowers emerge dramatically from green calyxes (the petal-like structures that grow just below the petals). The

(Text continues on p. 92.)

From its purplish-pink flowers to its purple pods and purple-green leaves, the hyacinth bean offers months of color for little effort. By taking advantage of vertical space, annual vines like this can expand even the smallest garden.

Photos, except where noted: Mark Kane; illustrations: Steve Buchanan

The small, snapdragon-like flowers of *Asarina scandens* (left) cover the plant in sensational profusion. The related creeping gloxinia (above) offers 3 in. blooms.

HOW VINES CLIMB

Recognizing how a vine climbs will help you decide how to support it. In general, both annual and perennial vines have evolved three ways of climbing up and over other plants: grasping, twining and clinging with adhesive discs or roots.

Many vines climb by tendrils—leaves or stems that are modified for grasping. Long and thin, tendrils try to wrap around anything they touch. Some coil like springs, while others loop over an object and then twine around themselves. Vines with tendrils can ramble vertically or horizontally, but they need supports that are thin enough to grasp. Vines that climb by tendrils include the common garden pea, cup-and-saucer vine, love-in-a-puff and the perennial sweet pea.

Some vines climb with their leaf stems (petioles), which coil like tendrils around small objects or each other. Among these vines are clematis, creeping gloxinia, purple bell vine and canary creeper. Often multi-stemmed, they cling to themselves as they climb supports or weave through nearby plants.

Another group of vines climbs by twining. Spiraling as they grow upward, they wrap their stems around plant stems and other thin, upright objects. Some species spiral in a clockwise direction, while others, such as cypress vine, morning-glory and moonflower, spiral counter-clockwise. Before a young twiner starts to climb, it moves imperceptibly from side to side or in a circle, seeking support. When it

Tendrils

Twining stems

The curious green fruit of love-in-a-puff lends a touch of the unexpected to the garden.

The sky's the limit for cup-and-saucer vine. It covers large fences or trellises and can speedily mask an unsightly view.

The variegated leaves and pinkish-brown flowers of morning-glory 'Chocolate' are a pleasing variation on a familiar vine.

contacts an object, it starts twining and growing rapidly. To train a young twiner onto a support, wrap it in the direction it turns naturally. Tie it to the support if needed and then let it grow unaided. A twiner can be coaxed in the wrong direction, but will soon let go.

The clinging vines climb in two ways. Some, such as Virginia creeper (*Parthenocissus quinquefolia*), produce tendrils that end in adhesive discs. The discs secrete a cement-like substance that fastens them to almost any kind of support, including bark, wood, stone, brick or masonry. They are good choices for covering walls, though it's a chore to strip them off once they are well established, and they can leave behind

Clinging roots

Clinging discs

persistently glued debris. Other vines, such as English ivy, climb by roots that form along their stems and hold on by clinging to a surface.

Vines need a support that matches their climbing habit. A disc-bearing vine, such as Virginia creeper, can scale a wall, while a twining vine, such as morning-glory, needs wire mesh, a lattice, treillage or the like. The hyacinth bean readily twines up a rustic tripod of cedar poles, but vines such as peas and grapes, which climb by tendrils, require supports of smaller diameter, such as open-mesh wire, netting, bamboo canes, thin stakes or finger-thick twigs known as pea brush. Both annual and perennial vines are capable of enormous growth during a growing season, but over many years, the perennials become much heavier, so be sure you start with an adequate support. **G.K.**

Photo, top left: Chris Curless

calyx splits open, becoming the "saucer," and the flower petals appear, fused into the "cup." Cup-and-saucer vine blooms profusely from midsummer until temperatures drop to around 25°F.

But beware: cup-and-saucer vine can easily grow as much as 20 ft. to 30 ft. in a season. One can almost see daily progress as it hoists itself upward. Be certain to give it a strong support—my sapling trellis came crashing down at the end of the season, done in by rot, the weight of moisture-laden foliage and a gust of wind.

Love-in-a-puff—Love-in-a-puff (*Cardiospermum halicacabum*) is a tendril-climber that hails from tropical climates. (See photos on p. 91.) More of a novelty than a showy ornamental, this plant is beautiful in its subtlety. Insignificant ¼-in. white flowers growing among coarse-toothed, alternate leaves are followed by inflated, balloon-like green fruit. At maturity, the fruit contains round, black seeds marked with a distinct, heart-shaped gray blotch, hence the common name. Plants like this one make for interesting conversation at a garden party and make me smile at the grand scheme of nature.

The hotter the summer, the faster love-in-a-puff grows and the more space it requires. (Other heat-loving annual vines respond similarly.) Planted in the ground, mine grew 6 ft. to 8 ft. tall; growing it in a container would keep it smaller. Love-in-a-puff's lacy foliage provides an ideal foil for the stiff, arching blades of an ornamental grass.

Morning-glories—Most people are familiar with old-fashioned single and bicolored morning-glories, cultivars of *Ipomoea tricolor*. Abundant flowerers, these colorful, twining vines give much in return for little effort. Flower colors include blue, purple, near-red, pink, white and combinations. The cultivar 'Heavenly Blue' is well-named and worth growing for its distinctive color (which turns a misleading pale purple in photos). Another striking cultivar is 'Chocolate', which has variegated leaves and pinkish-brown flowers outlined with white. (See photos on p. 93 and p. 91, respectively.)

For something completely different, I recommend a relative of the common morning-glory called cypress vine (*Ipomoea quamoclit*). It offers 1-in., intense scarlet, star-shaped flowers held among delicate, almost fern-like, divided foliage. Indigenous to tropical

America, this vine has a twining habit and grows 10 ft. to 12 ft. tall. Like all morning-glories, this one enjoys the heat of summer and blooms nonstop until fall frost. Before planting, nick the seedcoat with a file to improve germination.

Purple bell vine—The purple bell vine (*Rhodochiton atrosanguineum*) is an exotic-looking vine from Mexico and one of those plants whose exceptional form causes onlookers to fall silent for a moment while contemplating its intricate beauty. (See photo on the

The lobed leaves and small yellow flowers of canary creeper here complement the upright stems of red hot poker and the big yellow flowers of helianthus in the background.

SOURCES

The following mail-order nurseries each carry at least three of the annual vines described in this article.

J.L. Hudson, Seedsman, P.O. Box 1058, Redwood City, CA 94064. Catalog $1.

Park Seed Company, Cokesbury Road, P.O. Box 46, Greenwood, SC 29647. 800-845-3369. Catalog free.

The Thomas Jefferson Center for Historic Plants, Monticello, P.O. Box 316, Charlottesville, VA 22902. To request a seed list, send a postcard with your name and address.

Thompson & Morgan Inc., P.O. Box 1308, Jackson, NJ 08527. 908-363-2225. Catalog free.

W. Atlee Burpee & Co., Warminster, PA 18974. 215-674-9633. Catalog free.

facing page.) The 2-in. heart-shaped leaves are green with a delicate purple edging. Tiny buds nestled in the leaf axils develop into fuchsia-colored calyxes. A deep purple-black flower bud emerges from each calyx and elongates into a 2-in. long, pendulous, tubular flower with a flared rim. The flower and calyx make a colorful combination that lasts for several days. The calyx provides color for weeks after the flower is past its prime. From midsummer on, all stages of flowering cover the vine.

I planted purple bell vine in a 12-in. diameter terra-cotta pot, but you can also grow it in the ground. Trained onto a tripod of bamboo stakes, the stems climbed by coiling petioles to 3 ft. to 4 ft. high. You can bring containers of it into a sunroom or greenhouse for the winter.

Canary creeper—Canary creeper (*Tropaeolum peregrinum*, at left), a climbing nasturtium native to the Andes, bears little resemblance to the well-known garden nasturtium (*T. majus*). With some imagination, you can see how its 1-in. long, yellow flowers gave rise to its common name—the two upper petals of each flower are fringed and feather-like, while the three lower ones are narrower and smaller. The vine, which has attractive, medium-green, five-lobed foliage and climbs by coiling petioles, reaches 8 ft. to 10 ft. tall by fall. It likes half-sun, preferably in the morning. High temperatures seem to inhibit flowering. Last year, its yellow blossoms mingled with the scarlet fruit of my cotoneaster, creating a most satisfactory combination.

Care

Annual vines need little care. I fertilize and water them as I would most annual flowers. They don't require deadheading, and I've never had to spray them for insects or diseases. But they do require support and often some training to start climbing.

I start all of my vines from seeds under lights about two weeks to four weeks before I transplant them into the garden. There's no benefit to starting them earlier; if you do, you'll just have to contend with a mass of plants tangled all over each other. (In warmer climates, you can sow seeds outdoors.) I wait to set out vines of tropical origin until all danger of frost has passed and the nights have warmed up. Annual vines from more temperate climates can be set out earlier, about the last frost-free date. I sow most seeds in peat pots so I can set the seedlings into the garden without unpotting them and disturbing their roots.

Prop up fledgling vines with a bunch of twigs or a small bamboo stake to help them reach their permanent support. The first shoot may need a little coaxing to get a foothold, but then you can stand back and let the vine do the work. (If your vines are having trouble wrapping around wide supports, you'll need to tie them to the supports with string.) As the vines mature, a network of stems and leaves provides support for the new shoots to grasp onto. The occasional errant shoot can be gently tucked back in with the rest of the plant. If the vine oversteps its boundaries, just prune back the wayward shoots.

Choosing a support

Finding a structure to support annual vines is one of the most creative aspects of growing them. Fences, walls, trellises and poles are the most common supports, but the possibilities are unlimited. Last year, for example, I turned an old weather vane into a colorful sight by planting a mixture of morning-glories at its base. Other plants can serve as supports—annual vines can romp harmlessly over spring-blooming deciduous shrubs. A gardening friend commandeered her husband's espaliered pear to support and display a cup-and-saucer vine. Less vigorous vines can tumble over dwarf conifers— I've seen a beautiful combination of *Asarina scandens* scrambling up a golden variegated juniper.

As you choose a support, think about the options. Do you want a free-standing or attached support? Can you take advantage of existing fences or walls? What kind of structure will best complement the design of the garden? Do you want a temporary or more permanent support? Match the support to the vine's mature height and its climbing habit, and always make the support stronger than you think is needed.

The world of annual climbers is rich with possibilities. No matter what size garden you have or where you garden, there is an annual vine for you. This wonderful group of garden plants will never fail to provide continuous pleasure year after year. □

Gary Keim is a professional gardener who lives and gardens in Washington, Connecticut.

In striking contrast, fuchsia-colored calyxes shelter the tubular flowers of the purple bell vine.

An old favorite, 'Heavenly Blue' morning-glory reliably blooms through the heat of summer.

Index

The 18 articles in this book originally appeared in *Fine Gardening* magazine.
The date of first publication, issue number and page numbers for each article are given below.